The American Geisha

Judith Morland

authorHOUSE®

AuthorHouse™
1663 Liberty Drive, Suite 200
Bloomington, IN 47403
www.authorhouse.com
Phone: 1-800-839-8640

First published by AuthorHouse 7/28/2008

ISBN: 978-1-4343-8487-4 (sc)

Printed in the United States of America
Bloomington, Indiana

This book is printed on acid-free paper.

First, I wish to thank my chosen companion, my husband, Tom. Without his encouragement and patience, I never would have gotten past the first draft.

Secondly, I wish to thank my children, Patty for her input, Pamela for her input and her computer expertise, and Joseph for his financial help.

Third, I wish to thank my friends, Mitcheil Jackson, for her help with the delicate subject of sex games and Margaret Shaw whose curiosity and prodding kept me going and lastly my newest friend, Penny, whose excitement showed me that there is a need for this information.

Thank you all so much, I couldn't have done it without your help.

DEDICATION

To my mother, who taught me, through loving constructive criticism, how to be a lady and still be myself.

To my four children - may they not make the same mistakes that I did.

STROKES

The writer strokes with his pen,

His message to impart.

Hoping you will understand

The words within his heart.

The artist strokes with his brush,

Bright colors he will start.

Hoping you will understand

The visions in his heart.

The lover strokes with his hands,

The words he can't impart,

Hoping you will understand

The feelings in his heart.

-JMC 9/6/1993

THESE STROKES ARE FOR YOU!

YOU LIVE IN YOUR WORLD
AND I LIVE IN MINE,
IT'S ONLY THROUGH LOVE
THAT OUR WORLDS ENTWINE.
                    -JMC 10/07/1990

TABLE OF CONTENTS

INTRODUCTION

I first began The American Geisha when my youngest daughter was five years old. I hoped she would be able to read it when she became of age. Now, nearly fifteen years later, I'm reworking it. My daughter is twenty years of age, has just recently married, and already is the mother of two girls. My oldest daughter pointed out that married or not this information is helpful. You never know what the future holds in store for you and it's good to be well prepared.

The Webster's New World Dictionary (page 24, 1990) defines a 'geisha' as a "Japanese girl trained as an entertainer to serve as a hired companion to men." A true American Geisha must be that and much more. She must be taught self-esteem and self-confidence, but most importantly self-acceptance. She must choose her future carefully, to pursue a business, or to have and raise, a family or possibly both. Lastly, she must decide if she wants to go through life by herself or with a chosen companion. If she chooses companionship, she must be trained in the arts of providing for and serving her Chosen Companion. She must be taught, and be willing to give one hundred percent of herself. She must know herself first, then reach out for friendships, and then seek that special relationship with her Chosen Companion. She must be careful and consider all her options along the way. (We don't always get second chances.) A true understanding of human relationships comes from not only the desire, to have one, but a basic learning process as well. Anything worth having is worth working for. Your inner peace and peaceful relationships are the most precious things attained in this world and certainly worth every effort to attain them.

Please keep in mind, as you read this, that I am not different from any other woman. I have just allowed some bad experiences to push me into bettering myself, so I can more fully understand my own desires and have a better understanding of those around me. I sincerely hope that what I have learned can be of some help to those aspiring women, whether married or not, wishing a more perfect connection with her Chosen Companion and maybe have a better understanding of herself as well. This is only a personal guide, in relationships, to become a true AMERICAN GEISHA.

CHAPTER I

ABOUT YOU

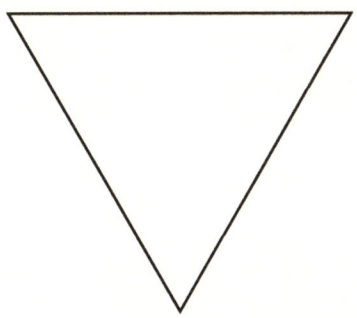

1. The Creation and Purpose of Woman

In the beginning, there was the Spirit, the Omnipotent, the Universal Force, the Supreme Being and the One, our Creator, God, the source of all. All elements of life, vibration, and matter are of this One Source. Vibration, life, and matter are of two principles, positive and negative forces. God's first creation was part of Himself, the Light or Life Force. This Light entity was separate but still part of the One. God granted the Light free will and thus, through the Light, our creation began. The first of creation were souls, or as we call them Angels, heavenly hosts and companions of God and the Light. After a time some of these souls deviated from the Light's and God's influences and became aligned with the angel Satan, who, as we all know, fell from the grace of God and was banished from Heaven. Next, it is written that God, in His wisdom, created the Universe and our own Earth. He then filled the Earth with life, both plants and the animals who ate them. After the Earth's creation, some of the souls were permitted to inhabit the creatures of Earth to experience life. Some of these souls managed their chosen creatures poorly so God created man and granted him dominion over all the creatures of Earth so they could be properly cared for and guided. The Light entered man, so he could be properly guided on the path to God.[1]

Man was the first and only one of his kind, thus he became lonely for a like companion. Finding nothing suitable among the animals, God caused man to sleep. While man, who had been named Adam, slept God took, from his side, a rib and from that rib, He created Eve, our first human woman. Actually, a man really has one less rib, than a woman, as confirmed by X-ray.

The important point is that woman was created to be a companion and helpmate for man. She is therefore, by creation, a helpmate, supporter, confidant and friend to man. She was not originally intended to rule over or be made a slave by man, but to take care of and be there for him. From his side she was taken to be his companion.

In the Garden of Eden, where man and woman lived, there stood two trees. They were called the Tree of Knowledge and the Tree of Life. God forbade man to eat of either one. Unfortunately, woman was tempted, by the snake, into eating an apple from the Tree of Knowledge. She shared it with her companion, Adam. When God found out, He banished them both from the Garden of Eden lest they eat of the Tree of Life. He cursed Eve, causing her to be ruled over by Adam and to suffer great pain of birthing his children. (Genesis 1:1 through 3:24; the Holy Bible)

Modern day Eves have pretty much returned to the state of the original Eve, before she was banished from Eden. We have become helpmates and caregivers, as well as companions, to our men. Of course, we still experience the great pain of child birth, but instead of being ruled over by man we've found it's better to help, serve and care for each other on a more equal basis. Both woman and man must have respect not only for each other but also for themselves as well. Whether you're the breadwinner or the chief-cook-and-bottle-washer, each should do their share. Lastly, modern day Eves need to know how to care for themselves should something happen to their Chosen Companion.

2. The Physical Body (Your Outer Self)

We were created by God, he breathed life into our body and gave us a soul. The physical body is therefore the house, or temple, of the soul. We need to take care of our body physically and mentally, so that it is clean and healthy for the soul to grow and thrive. Many religions teach us that through life, or many lives, we are given the opportunity to perfect ourselves, through soul growth, so that we may ultimately become one with God.

In order to accomplish this we must first look at ourselves, make needed improvements, maintain good body care and then teach our soul to love ourselves, others, our Chosen Companion and life. The best way to begin a personal makeover is to be very critical and brutal with ourself. Sit in front of a mirror and take a good, long look.

Exercise: Looking in the Mirror

To do this exercise you will need: a full-length mirror, or one with as much a view as possible; a straight back, but fairly comfortable, chair; and at least 45 minutes to one hour of undisturbed time.

The primary thought is in order to give love from oneself you must first accept and realize love of your self. Pull the chair in front of the mirror, sit in it and close your eyes. Take just a minute or two to calm yourself (a few deep breaths are all right) and shut out all the hectic surroundings that might interfere. This is the first of your time. Imagine a white heat, light, and vibration emanating from within. Do you feel it? This is your God-Spirit soul. We cannot touch it, but we can feel it burn within us, if we take the time to look and feel. This is the created life force, that once perfect soul still loved very much by the Light and our Lord God. Each one of us has one and it is through feeling this true inner beauty that we can come to accept our own worth. Open your eyes and look directly into the mirror. Look into your eyes, for they are the body's window to the soul. You should now begin to feel the spark of desire and self worth flowing within. Be proud, hold your chin up, you have a major purpose to be here, you are loved by God and you are one of His creations. Relax for a moment and take this all in.

Take a look at the larger reflection now. You may need a note pad and pencil, or pen, for this next part. Take a real good look at yourself. Keep in mind the 'ugly duckling' theory, no matter how 'ugly' you may feel, there can and will be a truly beautiful swan inside.

Still looking in the mirror? What do you see? What you see on the surface is the first impression other people get from you, your outer appearance. How do you feel about your outer appearance? Be brutal, with yourself and make notes. As your time provides look over your notes and work on them one at a time. Do not become overwhelmed at your task, it can cause stress, and stress is the worst thing we can allow our body to do.

Beginning at the top, your hair. Hair is considered 'woman's crowning glory'. It is her natural head covering before our Lord. Our hair is the one part of our body that shows the result of stress the most. Stress is the result of mental and/or physical tension, and strain, brought upon our body. Our hair demonstrates this by turning prematurely gray, or white, or by being 'mousey' dull looking. Dullness can also be caused by illness. Hair should not be flat or oily looking, but rather, bouncy and lustrous. Locate a good shampoo, being careful to read the label, in the event of allergic reactions. Maybe you wish to try a hair toner with the shampoo included. Use a good conditioner. Be sure to follow the directions on the bottles, or boxes, to get the best results. There is no real 'rule of thumb' on the amount of times you can shampoo, but as a general rule, don't color your hair more often than once every three weeks. I knew a lady, Barbara, who dyed her hair blond so often that it became brittle and dull. She'd rub mayonnaise on it and cover her head with a plastic bag for two hours, then rinse it off. She did have very shiny, soft hair immediately following this treatment. I don't know if I'd ever be brave enough to try it myself. However, I have heard of using a vegetable oil, such as olive oil, safflower or canola oil on hair. In between shampoos, if your hair lacks luster, you can put a drop, or two, of Rosemary oil on your hairbrush and brush it through to the ends. Incidentally, brushing your hair one hundred strokes a night is one of those 'old wives tales'. Depending on the length and condition of your hair, anywhere from twenty five to thirty five strokes should be fine. Brushing is not only good for your hair but it stimulates your scalp as well. Anytime you have problems, or questions, concerning proper hair care see a professionally accredited hairdresser/cosmetologist, that's why they're there. They can also give you advice on what hairstyle would be most flattering to your facial features.

Are you happy with the face returning your gaze? Our face is the next area most apparently reflecting stress. It displays stress in the form of wrinkles. "Crows feet" at the eye corners, comes with age but other facial wrinkles come from stress and worry. I feel that wrinkles are fine if you have earned them. They show a life of caring and worrying. You need to keep a positive outlook, turn the negative aspects into positive ones, and learn to laugh more. I have found a good simple facial once or twice a week will actually help tighten facial muscles and relieve wrinkles. It is not an over night cure. It took a while to get the wrinkles it will take a little time to ease them. For a quick facial try: 2 egg whites (separate the yolks out) and 2 drops of Rosemary oil; apply to face; allow to dry to crust - about 20 minutes - then rinse off.

Remember to wash your face at least two or three times a day to remove built-up dirt and oil. Good old soap and water are still the best. Do not wash your face so often as to cause it to become dry. If it does get too dry, use a good moisturizer. My mother-in-law, Gerry, applied Vaseline® every night. She did have a gorgeous face. Any problems with skin care, be sure to see a dermatologist. A healthy complexion should not be covered with makeup or cover-ups, other than a good sun block, during the day. My father taught me that your facial features should be enhanced by the makeup, so to use as little as possible. Choose makeup that goes with your skin tone and hair color. Sometimes, the girls at the cosmetic counters can guide you, and there's always the Avon Lady.

How about your overall body? Are you happy with your weight? Don't jump into a diet, talk to your doctor to see what type of diet is right for you, or if you even need to go on one at all. Being slightly overweight may be a sign of a slower thyroid gland. When I was 54 years old, I began putting on a little (too much) weight. First, I considered it as a result of the stressful times I was going through with my teenaged children, but even after I reduced the stress, I continued to gain weight. Funny thing though, I hadn't changed my eating habits. I finally became worried when I was pushing forty pounds over my regular weight and went to the doctor. Sure enough, tests revealed that I had a slow thyroid gland. With the help of medication, I now have enough energy to exercise, along with all my regular chores, and work off those extra pounds. In my case, a weight reducing diet wouldn't have helped, and I may have ended up depriving my body of what it needed. If you're just a little overweight and can't do anything about it - or are happy as you are - there are other things to focus on.

Dressing your body is important and when done properly will boost your spirits and self-esteem. They say that the clothes make the man. Well, it's clothes that also attract a man. A new dress is great for your morale, especially if it's one that deserves that second look or even better that 'wolf whistle'. If you can't afford a new dress, check your local thrift shops. They have many nice things and usually the money spent goes to a good cause. Choose comfortable clothes, as tugging at tight clothes never looks good. Under garments should also be comfortable. Tight fitting undies may look sexy but may be unhealthy. The biggest decision many women have is to wear a bra or not. Years ago, I was taught a simple trick with a pencil. Take a pencil; place it under each breast, one at a time. If the pencil falls, you don't have to wear a bra, but if it stays put, you need the extra support. Keep in mind that it is perfectly normal for one side to be slightly larger than the other is. If one side holds the pencil, while the other side does not, do wear a bra. As we all get older, our breast muscles sag, and good support early will lessen the sagging.

How you see yourself affects how others see you. Be confident, smile, walk with energy and purpose, choose clothes that reflect your personality, and remember you are God's child. Updating your wardrobe every once in awhile to keep with the times will help you feel younger. Don't worry about your height, bone structure, skin tone or age. You can't change some things and that's what makes us individuals. Change what you want to, and are able to change, but accept yourself for who you are.

Now put that mirror away!

3. Care and Feeding of the Physical Body

Grooming

Personal grooming, hygiene, is something that needs to be done on a regular basis, to care for and maintain your body. Things like brushing your hair, washing your face, and brushing your teeth need to be done twice a day. Taking a shower, or bath, can be done once a day, while shampooing your hair and manicuring your nails can be done once a week. Fit in the longer soothing bath as you have sufficient time to relax and enjoy it.

Brushing your hair twice a day keeps it tangle free and full looking. It also helps to distribute the natural oils from the scalp through the hair. Don't brush too vigorously or you will damage or break your hair. If brushing causes a static electricity buildup, put a small amount of hand lotion on your hands and run your fingers through your hair.

Washing your face once a day, is generally recommended, but if you live in a polluted environment or are exposed to extra dirt, you should wash it at least twice a day. Use a mild soap and don't rub it in so much that you clog your pours, just get the dirt off. Use warm water rather than hot. Rinse off good, leftover soap can irritate sensitive skin. In the evening, apply a good face lotion to replace lost moisture.

Everyone has their own comfortable way of brushing their teeth. The main thing is remembering to do it. The general recommended ways are: a circular motion on the front and sides; a back and forth motion for the flat molar surfaces and up and down strokes for the inside areas. Be sure to brush your tongue and the roof of your mouth. Lightly brush your gums. Trapped food particles in between teeth can cause bad breath and poor gum care can cause stomachaches. I wore braces, when I was young, and as a result, I had weak and receded gums. I also had lots of stomachaches throughout my life. On my fiftieth birthday, as a present to myself, I had my teeth and gums taken care of. Now a stomachache is a rare thing. Proper care of your teeth can save you dental visits. If you have good, clean, healthy teeth, you will smile with more confidence.

You should try to shower once a day, more often depending on your climate and the type of work you do. A cool shower can actually wake you up in the morning, but a shower that is too hot will dry out your skin. Use a body gel or mild soap. Pat dry afterwards and apply lotion to the dry areas.

Washing or shampooing your hair should be done on a weekly basis. If you wash it too often it will become dull and brittle.

While you're washing your hair, you can give yourself a manicure as well. Remove any old polish, wash your hands thoroughly, and then shampoo your hair. As you rub and massage your scalp, you will clean your nails and massage your fingertips. After you have conditioned, and rinsed your hair, towel dry it, then begin work on your hands and nails. File your nails according to your preference. It is generally recommended that nails should be no longer than one-quarter inch from the nail bed. This length reduces the chances of splitting and chipping and it is still a useful length. If you choose to apply polish, for longer lasting polish, use a base coat and finish with a top coat.

When your nails are dry, apply a good hand lotion, and massage your fingers and hands.

Activity Needs

In addition to personal grooming, your body needs a regular daily schedule of activities to stay fit and functional. According to my father-in-law, Jimmy, you should divide your day into three parts, eight hours each, of work, play, and rest.

Work and Play

Work includes the job you choose. You know, the one that pays to support you. Whether it's working in the home or away from the home, be sure that you choose one you like, not just one you're good at. Be happy in what you do. We all need to have money, but if you're unhappy, you will become depressed and stressed and your body's health will suffer. You will wind up throwing your money away on doctors. It's just not worth the trouble.

Play includes doing something that you like and, usually, getting the benefit of exercise while you're doing it. Exercise not only keeps us fit and trim but also increases our fresh air oxygen intake so it's great for your body. A good brisk walk is good exercise and, you never know who you might meet while you're out walking.

Rest and Sleep

After a hard day of work and play, begin your rest period by resting your feet. A good soak in a basin of warm (not hot) water will relax sore tired feet. Add a teaspoon of baking soda, a tablespoon of sea salt and a drop of your favorite perfume, or oil (I prefer Rosemary or Lavender oil) and soak for at least fifteen to twenty minutes. Wiggle your toes often. Your feet will love you. Rest also includes things you do to relax yourself. Rest is a time for body renewal, time to re-energize itself. You might take this time to put your feet up and read a book or watch television, listen to soothing music or even soak in a warm bath. A warm bath, just a little on the hot side, especially with a few drops of bath oil, is great for tense muscles, sore feet, a moisture loving body and personal relaxation. To a warm water tub, add 1 capful of fragrant bath oil or three to five drops each of Rosemary and Lavender oil. Rosemary oil is a natural muscle relaxer and Lavender oil sooths the senses. If you really want to pamper yourself, add one cup of milk and one teaspoon of baking soda to the warm water and oil mixture. While you're soaking in the tub, it's a good time to take stock in yourself. What are your dreams? What do you want out of life? Set realistic goals and start easy. There will be many baths. Keep in mind that you can't change your past but you can use bad experiences to make your present and future better. Give yourself credit for who you've become so far. Think of the good times and things, don't dwell on bad thoughts. Remember God loves you. There will be good times to come. After you've

> "With God all things are possible".
>
> Matthew 19:26
>
> The Holy Bible

relaxed and the water has cooled down and you've had time to ponder your life - get out. A nice fluffy towel feels great but pat, don't rub, dry. Apply a good body lotion to dry areas, and you're good to go. If it's late and you're planning to go to sleep, wait about ten minutes before retiring. Give your body time to adjust, have a soothing cup of tea, and then enjoy pleasant sleep.

Sleep of the physical body is your body's time for renewal and rejuvenation for the coming day. While your outer body is at rest, your internal organs have the time to repair, maintain, and replenish themselves. Nerves and muscles can relax and relieve tension while digestion can move on at a slower pace, so more nutrients are absorbed by your body. Sleep is the only thing, in the work-play-rest schedule, that can overlap into the others. If you don't consciously get the required amount needed by your body, your body will take it anyway. It's embarrassing when someone falls asleep at work, or at school, but it does happen. It becomes very dangerous when someone falls asleep at the wheel of a vehicle, but that also happens. Sleep requirements vary with age. Children, teens, and young adults may require up to ten hours, a night, while normally active adults usually require only eight hours, a night.

Older adults can usually get by on six hours a night, but are often plagued by insomnia and may take afternoon naps to compensate. Lack of sleep can cause tense muscles, fatigue and make you grouchy and irritable. If continued, lack of sleep can impair your response and thinking abilities. If it's time for sleep but you don't feel sleepy, read a book, or watch television. I get some of my best sleep in front of the television. Some people like a cup of warm milk before bedtime. Peppermint, catnip or lemon balm teas will also induce sleep. My father liked a bowl of cereal (milk) before bed, while my great grandmother insisted on catnip or peppermint tea. Don't go to bed until you are ready for sleep or you may lie awake and have interrupted sleep. Make sure you have a comfortable bed and that your pillows are positioned properly. If you have back or allergy problems, you may want to be propped up in a more upright position. If you have leg problems, elevate your legs or position a pillow under your knees. Whatever is the most comfortable for you will help you enjoy your sleep, and get the needed amount of rest.

Feeding

When we were in the Garden of Eden, God provided us with nutrition in the form of plants and fruit.

> "And God said, "Behold, I have given you every plant yielding seed which is upon the face of all the earth, and every tree with seed in it's fruit; you shall have them for food."
>
> Gen. 1:29 The Holy Bible

This was satisfactory nutrition for us then. After the great flood, God gave us permission to eat the flesh of animals, in addition to the fruit and plants. We not only got our nutrition from the fruit and plants but now second hand through the animals that ate them. Plus, we got everything that the animal had to offer. Our diet was once again sufficient. Unfortunately, in modern days due to the overuse, and abuse, of the land and product processing and refining, we don't get proper amounts of nutrients.

Even strict vegetarians, going back to our original diet of fruit and vegetables (grown organically, without pesticides, of course) don't get the vitamin B-12, a vitamin from all animal products, necessary for building genetic material and red blood cells. Unless you have your own, trained dietitian, you will need dietary supplements, for needed vitamins, minerals, and electrolytes.

When choosing a dietary supplement, be sure to read all labels. They are geared for all age levels and lifestyles. Age levels are: children, adult, pregnant/nursing adult, and senior adults. Lifestyles are for how active your body is or how much stress it is exposed to. Be sure the supplement contains vitamins, minerals, and electrolytes (potassium, sodium, and chloride). Some supplements also add phytonutrients, which are derived directly from plants. The word vitamin comes from the Latin word vita, for life, and amin, for amino acids, the body's building blocks. Vitamins are body regulators that are important for growth, reproduction, maintenance of health and proper body functions. In most cases, our bodies cannot make them so we must ingest them as our body uses them up. The one exception is vitamin D. The shining of the sun on our skin causes a chemical reaction, which in turn, causes our body to make vitamin D. Vitamin D is not necessarily ingested, but gathered as you stand in the sunshine. A well-rounded supplement should have everything you need in it. In times of extra stress, you may want to take additional amounts of B vitamins, called B-Complex. These will help you handle stressful situations better.

Be sure to eat plenty of red peppers, tomatoes, squash, and cantaloupes, as they are rich in antioxidants, needed for repair of cell damage. Eat plenty of fiber, found in wheat bran and whole cereals, for good digestive track health, and other high fiber foods, such as oat bran, beans, apples, and pears to help lower blood cholesterol levels. High fiber fruits and vegetables can help you avoid constipation and other intestinal problems. Of course, along with your food, you should drink plenty of water. It is generally recommended that the average person should drink eight glasses of water daily. If you're really active you should probably drink more. Water makes everything work. It cleanses the blood and body tissues of poisons and wastes. It also dissolves the nutrients so they can be used by your body, and it aids in regulation of your body's temperature. You can count the water in tea, coffee and fruit juices but the best is just plain ol' water. Too little water intake can contribute to kidney stones, cause headaches, fatigue and lack of mental alertness. So, eat good nutritious food and drink plenty of water. Take care of your body and it will take care of you.

4. Your Inner Self

> "For the Lord does not see as man sees;
> for man looks at the outward appearance,
> but the Lord looks at the heart."
>
> I Samuel 16:7 - the Holy Bible

The word heart, in the above quotation, does not refer to your heart organ but heart as in the center of your being, your soul. Your soul is the life force God gave us when He breathed life into man. The home of your soul is your inner self. Your feelings, emotions, dreams, hopes, desires, your appreciation of things (likes and dislikes), how you perceive life and your life energy, all emanate from your soul. If your soul is sick ('sick at heart') it will have devastating effects on your physical health as well as your mental health. In order to have a healthy soul you must learn to keep your feelings positive, your hopes and desires morally correct (clean thoughts), your emotions under control and your life energy flowing in a proper direction.

A quick check to see if you perceive life in a positive manner is how you consider a glass of water filled to the midline. Do you see it as half full or half empty? Half full would represent the positive outlook. You would be looking at life as full of expectations. My father taught me to look on the brighter side but to always consider all the aspects of the problem, just in case. You need to recognize the negative aspects in order to appreciate the positive ones.

Values, good morals, and religious beliefs, usually taught to us by family members, become part of our soul. Weighing these learned values and beliefs will help us to determine our self worth. Feelings and emotions often go hand in hand. For example, if someone insults your feeling of self worth you may feel hurt. Your resulting action, an emotion, might be to cry or strike back in anger. Before you strike back, consider the source of the insult. Perhaps the other person is full of negative, hurtful feelings. If you keep your feelings positive, the negative ones won't harm you. However, they may make you aware of any insecurity you may have. It will help you to 'get in touch' with yourself. Find these insecurities, or fears, face them and make them positive. When feelings and emotions are unbalanced, they can affect many body aspects: you can become 'cloudy', unable to make correct decisions; you may become lost and confused and you will become shaky, nervous and stressed, and possibly depressed as well.

Stress is the worst thing we allow our body, and inner self, to do. It weakens all our body functions, reduces our immune system (causing allergies and illness), dulls our hair, slows down our metabolism (causing weight gain), makes our nerves unsteady, and causes premature aging, all of which can cause depression. Everyone relieves stress in their own manner. My son, Joe, likes to walk it off. Sometimes, a good cry helps relieve it. You can just find a quiet moment, a quiet place, a comfortable chair, soothing music and just sit, relax and think happy thoughts. You might enjoy a cup of warm tea. Make it St. John's Wort herbal tea and it will lift your spirits. Whatever you do, don't let stress get you down. Remember you're not alone, God is there. If you do begin to stress over daily problems, consider the problems as challenges.

God gives us daily personal challenges so that we may overcome them and achieve personal soul growth.

As a child, and young teen, I was plagued with a multitude of problems. Most of them centered around the kids at school. I just couldn't fit in. I was, in my opinion, the world's worst 'ugly duckling' child. I had short red hair (no freckles), buckteeth, and my legs were too short. I wore braces (to correct the teeth) and then glasses. I don't need to list all of the cruel nicknames, other than to say that the list was probably longer than I was tall. The jeering isolated me from the other kids and I became a bookworm. My own feeling of self worth was so low, that I fell for the first good-looking man who had a kind word for me. I made the mistake of not discussing my problems with my parents. They probably could have helped me, but I just felt that they had too much going on in their own lives and I would just be a bother. Many years later, I've pretty much worked 'all the bugs' out. Well, at least I've accepted myself for who I am and that's the tallest hurdle. All improvement takes time. I have learned to face my problems one at a time, so I don't stress too much.

There is one major clue to realize your own self worth, a pet. I've always had dogs, but I never realized just how special they are. Our pets, particularly dogs and cats, but also birds and horses, love us for our own true self. They see with an inner eye. They see the kindness, gentleness, and goodness within us and love us without question. If I had recognized this earlier, I would have been spared a lot of pain.

If you have problems, if you find you can't handle the stress and no relaxing techniques help, you may become clinically depressed. Sad, mildly depressed moods are a common thing, we all have them. But, if you've had a loss or serious trauma and you become depressed for more than two weeks you may require medical help. Symptoms of depression include some of the following: sad, anxious, self-worthlessness, sleeping changes (too much or too little), no energy, unable to make decisions, cloudy thoughts, fast weight loss, or gain, and can't seem to get back in touch with reality. Sometimes it's nice to know that, once you're really down, the only way out is up. Things will get better it just takes time and patience. However, if you need the help don't be afraid to ask for it.

Certain Sleep

It could have been so easy,

They're just there in the drawer,

To take a small handful and

Sleep forever more.

But, the challenges of every day,

With obstacles to meet,

Require one must be substantial

Soul-ly on their feet.

-JMC 11/25/90

Please remember you're not alone. No matter how depressed you may feel there's a light at the end of the dark tunnel. Take the time to talk to God, it will make you feel better.

Meditation

Meditation, somewhat like relaxing from stress, is the way to get in touch with your inner self. To do this, you need a quiet place, dim lights, a relaxing smell of oil (lavender or rose works well) or incense, nice soft mood music (waves or pipes are good) and a chair or floor cushion. Sit straight, feet flat on the floor (if in a chair) and hold your head and neck upright. Rest your hands in your lap or on your knees. Begin to breath slowly, deeply and calmly. Focus on your breath as it moves in and out. Keep your mind free of distracting thoughts. Focus only on your breathing. Next, expand your focus around your body, becoming aware of it. As you become more aware, you will begin to feel your soul within. Look at it, feel your true inner beauty, your hopes and desires. After this experience, come back slowly. Focus again on your whole body then just your breathing. Take a few more deep breaths and slowly open your eyes. A nice stretch (and foot wiggling, if in a chair) helps close your session.

If you're interested in using meditation for self-improvement and body health, you may want to look into taking a class in Tai Chi or Yoga. Both use deep breathing and meditation along with exercise (and body poses) to improve the mind, body and soul. Then, there's that extra plus you might just meet someone nice who also shares your interest.

5. Your Home Environment

Your home should be your sanctuary, your safe haven from the outside world. It should reflect your likes and your comforts, what makes you happy and feel at ease. It should also contain something that stimulates growth. For example, a television is a tool that can relax you or teach you. A bookcase, full of a variety of books, will do the same.

The colors of your surroundings are also important. A well chosen color scheme for your walls can promote both rest and enlivenment. Color hues of blues and greens are restful and great for bathrooms and bedrooms. Lighter colors, yellows and peaches are good for living and eating areas. I also heard that light yellows and beiges are good for offices and dens. Softer colors like mauves can go most anywhere from the living room to the bedroom. The use of lighter shades will make smaller rooms look larger. Another thought is wallpaper. Old traditions, like Victorian, preferred wallpaper, particularly flowered ones. However, a wallpaper that is too busy can cause you to become nervous, so just do one wall. Of course, you can always go with white, or off white, walls and pick up the colors in throw pillows, furniture and drapes, or curtains. Paintings and pictures can also be used to set a mood. Water scenes (lakes, streams and ocean waves) or forest scenes will help put you at ease. Magical or mystical posters can add a certain flare to a bedroom wall. Keep your modern art for a den or office. Pictures of flowers, animals, and things growing or moving about will add cheer to smaller rooms.

The Chinese have an ancient philosophic belief known as Chi. Chi is the Life Force, the energy flowing in and around us and everything else. They arrange their homes so that the Chi may enter and leave in a positive flowing direction. This not only ensures the peace and harmony of the household but may also encourage a good flow of money as well. The Chinese achieve the optimum flow of Chi by arranging their furniture, and accessories, to attract or deflect the flow of Chi. The art of this arrangement is known as Feng Shui. Feng Shui uses the natural elements along with positive (yang) and negative (yin) forces with placement to bring balance and harmony into your environment to enhance the flow of Chi. Feng Shui is becoming more and more popular in our modern world as it brings us back into balance and relaxes us. Check out the waiting rooms in doctor's and dentist's offices. The best part of Feng Shui is that it can teach you how to balance yourself so you can live in harmony with the world around you. Even though you can learn the principles of this art from books, it is best to have a professional designer, trained in Feng Shui, to coach you.

If you can't go to the expense of a decorator or designer there are many home magazines available. Architectural Digest has lovely pictures of many room varieties. Whatever ideas you may come up with keep in mind you're decorating to feel safe and comfortable. You will be spending many hours in your home.

6. The Whole You

When I was separated from my first husband, I spent some time volunteering at the church my grandfather went to. The minister counseled me for depression. He also taught me the theory of the triangle. Each of us is a triangle, with three aspects. In order for you to become whole, you must understand each aspect of yourself.

Your first aspect is your outer appearance. It is how you present yourself to the world and other people. It is not only your physical appearance but also your confidence, forthrightness and mannerisms.

Your second aspect is your inner self. This includes your dreams, hopes, desires, your likes and dislikes, what makes you happy, your moral and religious beliefs. With the exception of an occasional display of emotions, this side is usually hidden.

Your third aspect is sex. This is what you are, female or male, your preferences, your lusts, urges and cravings.

SO, thus the WHOLE YOU:

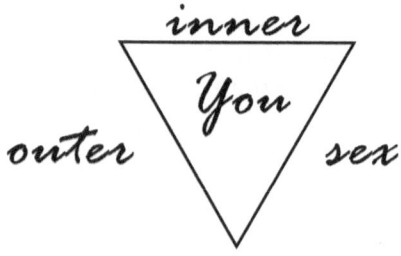

Now imagine yourself as a triangle and each person as an individual triangle. The next important lesson was, even though no two people are exactly alike, in order to have a relationship, of any type friendship or permanent companion, you must have at least two sides of your triangles in common. Sometimes we are lucky enough to find another person with all three sides, of the triangles, in common. We will feel especially drawn to this person, they are our soul mate.

Judy's Instructions

Walk the line, but be careful not to cross over.

Don't mistake friendship and caring for something else.

Do not let your situation make you vulnerable.

Hold on to reality.

The line between friendship and love is fine.

Do not mistake a physical need for emotional fulfillment.

When it is there, this time the feelings will be felt by both of you.

This time, love should not be only one sided.

You are a worthwhile person.

You are a child of God.

Hold onto your head, but more importantly Hold on to you heart.

Keep focused.

True love will, and must come.

Patience is a virtue and you are worth it.

-JMC 7/31/91

So, taking into consideration all that you have read so far, you should now be able to go out there and find your friends, lovers and that special someone, your chosen companion. Be careful. It's a jungle out there. There will be many people also searching. Keep a positive attitude to protect yourself from harm. It always helps to have a plan. Do you want a friend? Do you just want a fling? Or do you want commitment? Whatever you decide, good luck and may God go with you.

The Triangles

The actual drawings I've taken for the triangles are from a book on esoteric astrology, specifically used for their sizes. The triangles are symbols from the shades of time, before the written word. They were used to symbolize the male, as an upright triangle, and the female, as an inverted triangle. When you combine the two, for a couple, you get the six-pointed star, which was also in use before the Star of David. The triangle symbol also fits nicely with the triangle theory.

I originally wrote this text with my daughter in mind so the whole you is represented as the inverted and feminine triangle.

Thus, we have:

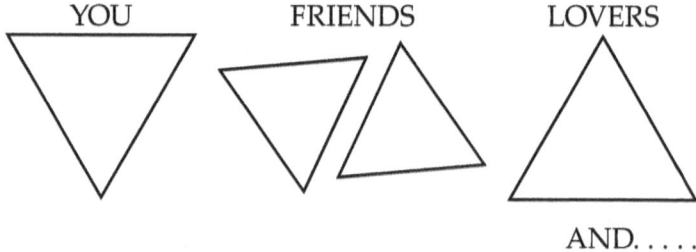

YOU   FRIENDS   LOVERS

AND. . . . .

THE BLENDED COUPLE - YOU AND
YOUR CHOSEN COMPANION

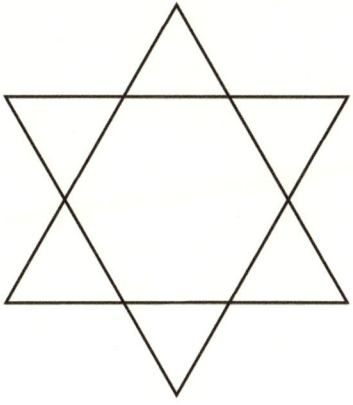

CHAPTER II

ABOUT THEM

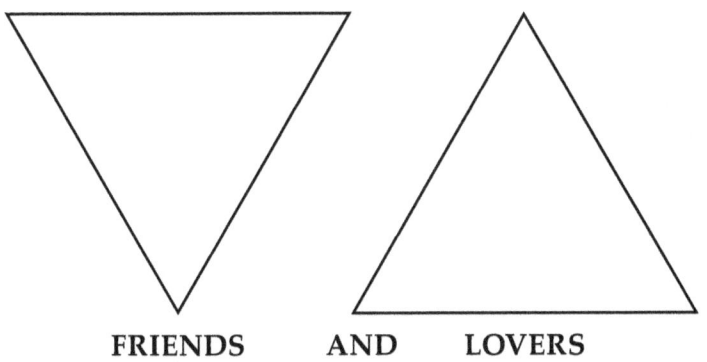

FRIENDS   AND   LOVERS

Chapter II ABOUT THEM

To have a friend, to be able to bond with another person is a gift from God. He created the first woman, Eve, as a friend and companion to the first man, Adam. They were friends first and they knew nothing about sex, and reproduction, until Eve's encounter with the snake, followed by banishment from Eden and God's curse on Eve.

Friendship is when two people, after having met each other, find that they have something in common - one side of their personal triangle. If they choose to get to know the other person, through conversations and spending time together, they may find that they have more in common - two sides of the triangle. They now become good friends.

> "A friend loves at all times."
>
> Proverbs 17:17 - The Holy Bible

A casual lover can evolve from either of these two stages of friendship. It may be just a one time 'hop in the sack' affair (sex side only) or it may be something more intimate shared by good friends (at least two sides of the triangle). Either way be careful not to mistake a physical urge for lasting emotional involvement. A friend of mine once said, "Men are like dogs." She's right. Dogs do it anywhere, anytime and with anyone. Then, they hop right off and leave with no lasting ties. Men are motivated by the physical urge for sex, once it's over so may they be. Such are casual lovers, but sometimes even they help bolster self-esteem. At least someone was there for a little while.

It is said, that 'birds of a feather flock together'. Please choose your friends wisely, they may be around for a long time.

Friendship is not limited to sex. That is to say, your good friends - even your best friend - can be either your same sex or of the opposite sex. It is also not limited to age, some good friends are many years apart. And, you don't need to limit the number of friends, you may have many.

Never take a good friend for granted, they are special. To have a good friend, one must also be a good friend. Good friends respect each other's feelings. It is important to know that all good relationships are based on respectful love and open, honest communication. Do not lie to your friend. Good friends don't lie to each other. There is a silent promise of truth between good friends. If that promise is broken, so often is the friendship. If this happens and you cannot mend the friendship, move on. You'll make more friends just don't make the same mistakes.

A best friend friendship is a little different from that of even a good friend. With a best friend, you can bare your soul. A best friend will be there for you all the time; through thick and thin, good times and bad. They will be there to help you up and hold you up. They will be there to laugh with you as well as cry with you. A best friend knows the real you and sees the beauty within, providing you are open enough to allow it. They will also listen to your problems with a caring ear. Even if they can't help, at least they've listened and that alone helps. Your best friend, will most likely, have in common at least two sides of your personal triangle. If, however, your best friend happens to be of the opposite sex, it's always possible they could share the third side (sex) and eventually become your chosen companion. If not just enjoy this special friendship. But, if there is a good possibility, carefully cultivate and nurture this relationship, a total three-sided triangle is rare and very special.

We've been together once,

We may never be again.

But that won't stop my loving you,

I'll always be your friend.

We have a special understanding.

For me that's very rare.

To know you'll always be my friend,

To know you really care.

I'll always be there for you,

In all you say and do.

It's part of being a friend,

It's part of knowing you.

To me there's a tender side

Still deep within my heart.

Tho' lovers go their separate ways

True friends never part.

-JMC 2/27/1992

Locating Friends

The key to begin locating your friends is within yourself. Know yourself to find out what you have to offer a potential friend. In the 1970s, it was fashionable to introduce one's self with the line, "What sign are you?" Of course, some people did use it as an approach but there were those who were really interested in making a deeper connection. Read up on your astrology sign, at least your Sun Sign, the one for the month you were born in. The information may just hit home and increase your self-awareness. One of the best astrology books available is <u>Sun Signs</u> by Linda Goodman. Besides reading about your own sign, you can read about friend's signs, if you know their date of birth. Learn about your own sign first then search for friends with compatible signs. You will be happier in the long run if you do this. There are two things you have to be careful about: l. Opposites sometimes attract. I have had some very personal experience with this. My first husband was a Scorpio, a water sign with passions to the extreme, and I am an Aries, a fire sign and very headstrong. Water puts out fire and he definitely did just that. I became what is known as a 'crushed' Aries; 2. Choose your like signs for friends and even good friends, but for a chosen companion, your same sign might be too much of a good thing. Too much the same may cause conflicts.

Just in case you're wondering how the sun could affect you, think about the moon. We can all see the affect of the moon on our earth, it's called the ocean tides. The sun being larger even though farther away, exerts the same type of pull on us, since we are at least seventy per cent, or more water (scientists are still working on this figure). The major influence exerted on us at the time of our birth caused us each to have specific traits.

The term Sun Sign means in what celestial zone the sun was in at the time of your birth. This is the sign of the month you were born. There are twelve one-month periods, one sign corresponding to each time-period. Each sign falls into one of four categories of fire, earth, air, and water. Your like signs are your best bet for good friends. A sign that you need (for example fire needs air OR earth needs water) would be your second best choices. Try it out, see if it works for you.

Fire Signs	Aries, Leo, Sagittarius
Earth Signs	Taurus, Virgo, Capricorn
Air Signs	Gemini, Libra, Aquarius
Water Signs	Cancer, Scorpio, Pisces

It's OK to let your heart lead you but let your mind advise you. It never hurts to have extra knowledge.

Where to go to look for a friend is always a fun problem. Perhaps you still have some friends from school around. A rule of thumb is: Never go to a bar unless you want to catch a barfly. Although, it might be just the place to find a 'one night stand'. For more serious relationships, you need to find, and join, a group of people with shared interests. There are always ads in the papers for single groups, also Parents Without Partners groups, that are local. You might try a library or a health club. I used to strike up conversations with people at the Laundromat, or while standing in line at the grocery store. If you're young enough, go to college. You're bound to meet someone there and you already have a class as shared interest. You might even join a poetry club, always tender hearts there, and if you're in a small town try a local church. Take plenty of time to look around. There are many potential friends out there. As far as men, there seems to be plenty of them available as well. Watch out for the married ones just looking for a good time - unless that's what you want.

I Will Not Be Afraid

I will not be afraid to give.

For it is through giving that we learn

To share God's gift of love,

Thereby enriching our own lives.

I will not be afraid to learn.

For it is be keeping an open mind that we

Are able to attain knowledge to enable

Ourselves to live to the best of His expectations.

I will not be afraid to feel.

For it is through our feelings, for each other,

That we can experience happiness as well as sorrow.

Without emotions, there would be a great emptiness.

I will not be afraid to love.

For God placed that feeling within our beings

So that it might be shared with all His creations

Including mankind.

AND

I will not be afraid to love,

Even if it hurts.

For the experience itself

Will be worth the pain.

-JMC 10/20/1991

We all need the gift of friendship. Sharing with a good friend will keep you from being depressed, which in turn keeps you happier and healthier. It is important to have a good family, but just as important to have a good friend. You can share things, with a good friend, you'd never tell your family. The more you have in common with your friend the longer the friendship will last. Do not be afraid to search for a good friend and when you find one, do not be afraid to enjoy the friendship.

Keep a stiff upper lip! Go out there and meet someone. Remember the triangle theory, throw in a little astrology, and find those good friends, a companion and maybe a lover or two to boot.

Go on a Man Hunt

Don't be afraid to check out the opposite sex. Guys aren't the only ones who can enjoy the hunt. Take your time and look around - and up and down. Go to a place where many people gather and do some comparing. There are certain things to look for. Just the way a guy wears his hair, or how his hands are can tell you what he's like. If nothing else, take a friend with you and have some good laughs.

According to psychologist, Elayne Kahn, the way a man parts his hair can say a lot about his personality: A right side part means he's practical and orderly; A left side part means he's a non conformist, creative, artistic and independent; A middle part means he's a middle type looking for balance emotionally and politically; A far right or far left part means he's courageous, outspoken and doesn't care what others think about him; A changing part means he's spontaneous and seeks new adventures, he needs a lot of excitement in his life; A part different from the natural one means he's not satisfied with ordinary things, always striving for improvement; and no part means he's carefree, very spontaneous, happy and relaxed.[2] So now, you know that having a part means much more than just that he is a mama's boy.

We've all heard that hands tell tales as well. The rule is his hands will be in proportion to his sexual equipment. In other words, if you're looking for that possibly well-endowed man, look for one with long fingers. But, there's much more...Sally Fry and Rosalind Craig, authors of a book called <u>Destiny</u>, made quite a study of general traits of man and his hands. Beginning with the thumbs and working through the fingers: 1. The thumbs - a long thumb a man who wants to impress others; a thin thumb shows a man who is cold and distant; a thumb shaped like a cone indicates an impulsive man and those with thick thumbs are over bearing; 2. The index finger - a pointed one shows the man is bossy; an extra big one shows ambition; 3. The middle finger - a man with a long middle finger may be very serious but, if the middle finger bends toward the index finger he may have problems facing life; 4. The fourth finger - if it bends toward the middle finger he may be unrealistic and guilty about love; 5. The little finger - this finger reveals possible sexuality problems. If it's low set into the palm there may be a parent fixation, which can lead to bedroom problems. If it bends toward the palm it is an indication of prudishness and it it's held away from the other fingers he may avoid commitments. The authors also say that if a man has hairy backs of his hands it means he's sexy with a passionate nature.[3] What more can you want? Now we'll all run out and check for those men with hairy hands.

How he holds your hands is another indication of how he is, or will be. If he holds hands with his fingers entwined with yours he'll be very tender and loving but if he holds your hands too tightly it may be a sign of insecurity, that he's afraid he'll lose you. The hand authorities also point out that if his palms are unusually sweaty it may mean he's prone to liver or kidney disorders and may have ill-balanced moral natures. Dry palms indicate a man who can develop a temperature easily, red palms mean a violent nature, pale palms mean he is selfish and smooth palms may mean he's prone to rheumatism. Not all palm information is bad; they do say that a pink, slightly mottled skin, palm means he's cheerful and has a well balanced personality. So now, we have long fingers with hairy-backed hands and mottled pink, not sweaty but not too dry, palms. You now have some idea where to begin looking and who to look for. So what are you waiting for? Get going. Find someone you can laugh with, it will make life's problems easier to handle.

JUST A NOTE

Up to this point, I have only mentioned your chosen companion as just that - not necessarily male or female. In modern times, the sexes can be somewhat confused. The traditional man-woman relationship is not always the case. Whatever your choice is, you must be true to yourself. The well-being of your soul must always come first for your personal happiness. One cannot have peaceful relationships if one has no inner peace.

From this point on, since I have always been in the traditional relationships, other than friends and best friends, I will be writing from that perspective.

Finding Your Chosen Companion

God may have created woman to be with man but He did not specify which one, or give us a map to find

41

the right one. However, He did give us certain feelings of attraction toward others. Sometimes you will feel drawn to someone, a feeling more powerful than just a sexual urge. When you meet this someone, be slow and carefully research him. Watch his eyes when he speaks. Normal facial responses can be somewhat controlled but not the eyes. Remember the saying 'the eyes are the windows of the soul'. If he looks you in the eyes as he speaks, he's interested in you. Don't be afraid to ask questions and be a good listener. This way he'll know you're interested in him, and what man doesn't love to talk about himself. Remember the triangle theory, search his sides. Find out what makes him tick before you start pushing his buttons. If he becomes distracted and starts looking around he's losing interest. Change the subject of conversation or move on. Life's too short to spend too much time on the wrong guy.

If you are able to hold his interest on the first meeting, you are now ready to move to the next step - sharing time together. Now, it's time for serious research. Find out what makes him happy, what makes him laugh and what he wants for his future. Suggest doing simple things like a walk in a park or sitting on a bench under a full moon. Watching the sunset is also good, especially with dinner. I used to like going up on a hill to park the car and look out at the city nightlights or just star gaze. This gives, you a different outlook at your world and creates a feeling of peace at the same time. This is a very nice thing to do especially after a long hard day with screaming children. Keep the conversation going, don't let things get too quiet. You need the research time.

Once you've become close friends the topic of sex can come up. Be sure you are both clear on your

> The man who loves me will have to know,
> True love out of friendship must grow.
>
> -JMC 2/27/1992

intentions. He still may be playing you along just to 'hop in the sack'. If that does happen and it's good, see what the next few days bring. Don't push him. Men like to be in control (or at least think they are). If he doesn't call to see you again just chalk it up to experience and move on. It may hurt your pride a little but you will survive and, there's plenty more fish in the sea. If he does call and you begin a serious relationship, good for you. Once you have made that commitment to each other and you move in together, a whole new life will open up for you. You now have your Chosen Companion, take care of him.

CHAPTER III

ABOUT YOU AND YOUR CHOSEN COMPANION

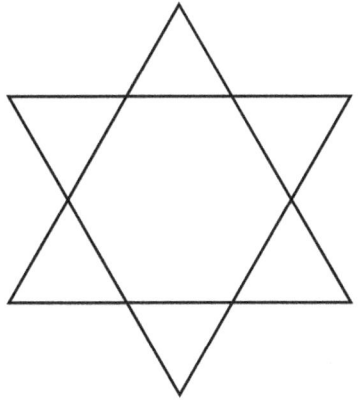

Chapter III You and Your Chosen Companion

You can fall in and out of love many times, even with many companions. If you're lucky, you will find one that will last many years. If 'love makes the world go round' then laughter is the music for love's dance. Having a companion that you can laugh with will help you through life's tougher times. If you do find yourself in a bad relationship get out, as soon as possible, and as gracefully as possible - bitterness makes enemies. Remember that nothing lasts forever. Even life long companions, are eventually separated by death. It's not necessarily the quantity of life, but the quality of life you share together.

Imagine your life, together, as a journey down a road. The straight, smooth areas are your happy times your comforts, stability and your good health periods. The warning signs are the DON'Ts, if you do them it will cause problems (the potholes). The scenic views and routes are the really happy times, the special things and the shared DO's (do this and you'll be happier) in your life.

Life is not perfect, nor would we want it to be. You have to have some bad in order to appreciate the good. If you tackle your problems, together, as they arise, turn them into a challenge, and work through them, they won't be as bad. You will learn to face life as a team and it will bring you closer together.

1. Care and Feeding of Your Chosen Companion

Hopefully, Chapter I has taught you how to live in your world. Once you have made a commitment to, and moved in with another, you need to learn to live in their world as well. It might be helpful if you sit down and map out both the personal triangles. List all the things you know about each other, likes and dislikes, things you both enjoy and all the things you have in common. Discuss things from what you like to eat, what activities you like to how you wish to decorate your home together. Don't assume that the cooking and cleaning chores are those of the woman. Many men like to cook and clean. It doesn't matter who does them, they just need to be done. There are some men, who do feel that if they work eight hours a day, they don't have to do any chores. In this case, you will have to accept this or reject the relationship. It's best to get some things worked out early so you'll know what's expected of you.

Care of your companion falls into two categories, physical and mental care. Physical care is: making sure his nutritional needs are met; encouraging proper grooming habits; body care such as foot rubs and back massages; and taking care of his sexual needs. Mental care involves mostly stroking his ego.

Many nutritional requirements are the same in both men and women, so review Chapter I part 3. A normally active man may require a multiple vitamin, in addition to good nutritious food, to ensure plenty of A, B and E vitamins, the mineral zinc, trace nutrient manganese and electrolytes potassium and sodium, to insure a good healthy sex life. Two tablespoons of honey everyday is also good for his sexual appetite. In fact, two tablespoons of honey may help you as well. As they age, men and women also have separate additional requirements. Women have a tendency for osteoporosis (thinning bones) and require more calcium. Men, because of an abundance of testosterone, have tendencies toward high bad cholesterol and prostate gland enlargement. They also are at risk for heart disease and high blood pressure. Make sure they have a diet rich in fruits, vegetables (fresh are best), seafood, olive oil and whole grains. Eating garlic and onions will help lower high blood pressure and reduce bad cholesterol. Ginkgo biloba, an herbal antioxidant, is good for blood circulation. As they get older men may also require an increase in fiber intake, supplement with Metamucil® or Benefiber® for psyllium, for constipation problems. Also, if they get ulcers, give aloe vera juice to heal and soothe with peppermint tea. Lastly, if prostate gland problems occur, have your man see a doctor. You can supplement with saw palmetto (an herb) if you notice problems with frequent urination, but if the gland becomes enlarged, professional help is definitely needed.

Encouraging regular, proper grooming habits can be a touchy subject. Beware of telling him that he stinks. It's much nicer to suggest taking a shower together and much more fun. Be sure you compliment him, once in awhile, on his choice of clothes or you'll be laying them out all the time. Shaving is another touchy subject. If you prefer him clean-shaven, tell him that his smooth face turns you on. Similarly, if you prefer him with a mustache, or beard, tell him that turns you on. Some men will even be flattered if you suggest that you shave them. Make sure you buy him two bottles of shaving lotion, one that he likes, and one that you like to smell on him. Fingernail care is optional with a man. Most men feel that nail care is a 'female thing'. My third husband, J.B., permitted me to file his chipped nails twice a month, but he drew the line at protective clear polish.

When your man comes home from work, give him time to unwind. Offer him a relaxing tea, or coffee if preferred. There are beverages and teas to suit almost every need. If he's tired and wants to rest there's a tea for that, or if he wants a quick 'pick me up' there's one for that. Don't be afraid to ask what he wants, it shows you care. If he asks for tea choose from the list below for the appropriate situation. Herbal teas may be purchased from Health Food Stores. Some simple already prepared, in bag form, herbal teas can be found in some of the larger grocery stores. Read the label to check the ingredients. Boil the water, pour over the tea bag, and let steep for five to seven minutes.

For a Quick Pick-up (Stimulant): teas made from cayenne, elder, prickly ash, peppermint, ginger, cloves, red sage, raspberry, nettle, and St. John's Wort.

Sexual Stimulant: Ginseng (don't use if high blood pressure), plantain, fenugreek, jasmine, saffron, savory and saw palmetto.

Relaxant: chamomile, hops, motherwort, mullein, vervain, skullcap, peppermint, and catnip.

Sexual depressant: black willow, hops, sage, skullcap, star grass and Wild Oregon grape.[4]

You have to judge for yourself on his actual requirement for back and foot rubs. Don't spoil him too much! If he has back problems he may not even want to be touched, but if his back is just sore from work, a regular massage may be needed. If he's real tense and sore, suggest a warm bath first. Many men suffer from migraine headaches, because of daily stress. A gentle scalp and forehead massage may relieve headaches. After all, women are the ones supposed to have the corner on headaches. For a regular maintenance massage, have your companion lie on a pad on the floor and you kneel along side. Begin by stroking in rhythmic flowing movements. Slow stroking is calming, while fast stroking is stimulating. To relieve muscle tension use direct pressure, with both hands flat, one on each side of the spine. Start at the lower back and work up to the shoulders, applying gentle but steady pressure. Use kneading (as in kneading bread) motions for the shoulders and neck. Finish with gentle stroking of the entire back area.

Rubbing the feet is its own form of massage, known as Reflexology, but in a mild form. There are thousands of nerve endings in the sole of the feet. The idea is that the feet are a reflection of the body. Imagine the sole of the foot, the toes as the head and the rest follows. The right foot covers the right side of the body, both back and front. The left foot, the left side of the body, back and front. The tops of the feet are the back of the body and the soles are the front, the inside arch area is the spine. The outer edge of each foot is the outer edge of that side of the body. Did you know that by massaging the big toe you can relieve sinus congestion or by massaging the neck of the big toe you can relieve a stiff neck? Before you begin rubbing the feet, have your companion soak them, or you can wash them yourself with warm water and a washcloth. If the feet smell, put a little baking soda in the water. Gently towel dry them. It's usually best to massage one foot at a time. Use your fingers and thumb to apply gentle pressure to specific areas of the foot to release stress and promote relaxation. For best results, pay most attention to the base of the toes, the base of the ball of the foot, down the outside edge, and where the arch area becomes the heel. End with applying a nice body lotion. You may want to buy a book on Reflexology to study up on different techniques.

You need to discuss your companion's regular sexual requirements early on. Don't assume that he wants 'it' all the time. In a new relationship, he may feel the need more often. Once a day may be considered normal, some feel the need only once a week. If he's working, he may be tired, and rather than risk a poor performance, go without until a day off. With a man, it's a physical need and it needs to be taken care of when the need arises, otherwise it can have painful results for him. With a woman sex is more a mental and emotional thing and it takes a little more time. Save your longer lovemaking sessions for the weekend, when you have more time to relax and enjoy it.

A certain amount of mental care of your companion is also required. This type of care is a form of stroking. This type of stroking is not the rubbing you give a pet, or his back, but more a touching of his soul. Everyone needs this stroking, and if you give out plenty you will receive plenty. Stroking can be anything from a cheery hello, to kisses and hugs and the final "I love you" at the end of the day. Cater to your companion. My husband, Tom, likes his cup of coffee first thing in the morning, so I bring it to his bedside when I wake him. If your companion works, don't forget to tell him that you love him and to have a nice day. Be home when he gets there, an empty house can be depressing to come home to. Give him unwinding time before rushing the meal and afterwards, leave the dishes and spend some quality time with him. When it's time to go to bed, tell him, again, that you love him. It's said that, couples who say, "I love you" more also have sex more often and are happier. If you stroke your companion properly, you'll hear a satisfied purr, in more ways than one.

Your overall home together should reflect both your likes. However, you should each have at least one room, or area, for yourself. For example, I have an office and Tom has a shop. Everyone needs a little space for them self. This particular area should be decorated in the manner preferred by its occupant. The rest of the rooms need to reflect both of you. The living room should reflect both more equally than say the kitchen. The kitchen should be decorated by the one who spends the most time in it. For example, if you're doing the majority of the cooking, you choose the colors of the walls, the curtains and even where the pots, pans and cooking utensils go. Choose soft colors for the bathroom and bedroom, to induce relaxation. Light pink and lavender work for bathrooms while blues and greens are better for bedrooms. Use lighter colors for small rooms it makes them look larger. Use mirrors to reflect light in darker areas. Be sure to discuss the decorating ideas together. Talk over wall colors to accent colors of furniture and pillows. Choose pictures together. Look over decorating magazines for ideas. If you have money, you may wish to hire a decorator or even a feng shui practitioner, to bring balance and harmony into your home. Remember your home is your safe place, and now it's a safe place shared by two.

2. The DON'Ts

There will be times that you just can't help yourself you'll do something you know you shouldn't do. This is a DON'T. They are things that women do that men don't like. It is best to avoid them, as much as possible, like the potholes in the road.

A. Don't be a gold digger - your companion wants you to love him for himself not for his money.
B. Don't be jealous - Although your companion might be flattered that you're jealous, it is an issue of trust. If you don't trust him, why are you with him?
C. Don't nag - Nagging is a form of putting him down. Remember you need to stroke him.
D. Don't hang on him too tight - Don't depend on him for everything. You're grown-up; make some of your own decisions.
E. Don't dwell on past relationships - He may think that you're unhappy with him. Besides how would you feel if he brought up all his old girl friends?
F. Don't whine - Whining gets old fast. It will make him feel inadequate.
G. Don't do drama - He probably has enough drama at work, he doesn't need it at home too.
H. Don't gossip to him - That's what girl friends are for. Unless the gossip affects him, he probably won't understand it anyway.
I. Don't overdress, when you go out together, unless it's formal attire. You are there to compliment him, not out shine him.

J. Don't push him - Men like to be in control, or at least think that they are.

K. Don't let problems build up - Handle them one at a time.

L. Don't shirk your responsibilities - If it's your chore to clean the house (and feed the pets) do it.

M. Don't sweat the small things - They're not usually as bad as you think they are. Take care of them yourself.

N. Don't push him into marriage - A good relationship is much better than a bad marriage. Don't rush into it if you're not ready. Some men treat the marriage license like a fishing license. They think it gives them ownership of you and they have the right to abuse you.

**THIS PAGE IS FOR YOU TO LIST ANY
DON'TS YOU MIGHT ADD.**

3. The Dos

I'm sure, as you go along, that you'll find more DOs, but these are some of the important ones:

A. DO learn to give of yourself - Always give one hundred per cent of yourself in everything that you do, but especially in a relationship. If you do this, no matter how the relationship works out, you will never have any regrets or doubts about your part in it.

B. DO keep communication going - Communication plays a part in every relationship, be it friendship or companionship. There are two forms of communication, non-verbal and verbal. Between friends, non-verbal signs are waves, smiles, and winks. Companions and lovers share a more intimate type involving body language. They demonstrate this by how close they stand, how often and where they touch, hug, or put an arm around each other. Other signs are gentle shoulder rubbing, a pat on the head or a quick kiss on the forehead. When conflicts do arise, verbal communication becomes necessary, so you can be sure where each of you stands. Work through your conflicts calmly. Try not to get loud or argue. Many cruel things can be said during a heated argument. Once said, even though not meant, they cannot be unsaid. Keep in mind that the basis of any good relationship is open and honest communication.

C. DO practice the four T's: Truthfulness, Tolerance, Tenacity, and Tenderness - Always be truthful with yourself and your companion. If you are truthful with each other there will never be any question of trust AND, you'll never have to try to remember what lie you told. Tolerance is acceptance of yourself, first, then of your chosen companion. Everyone has flaws. That's what makes us individuals. Some of these flaws will change as the relationship grows. You can learn to tolerate those that don't change. Learn to love your companion flaws and all. Tenacity is the holding on. No matter what problems arise, they can be talked out to a mutual agreement or they can be forgiven. A lasting relationship sometimes takes a lot of work. A relationship only fails when one quits working at it. Don't be that one. Tenderness falls into the non-verbal form of communication shared by companions and lovers. Tenderness can also be displayed in the caring things you do for each other, bringing a cup of coffee first thing in the morning, preparing breakfast in bed or buying something just because your companion likes it. Tenderness is showing that you care without expecting anything in return.

D. DO try to settle all problems before going to bed -

> "Do not let the sun go down while you are still angry."
>
> Ephesians 4:25 – the Holy Bible

Always try to work out any problems before going to bed you'll sleep better. I shared this with my third (and late) husband. I thought it might be because he was so much older than I that he thought he might die in his sleep before he had a chance to patch up an argument. It may have been that as well, but he also needed to have a settled mind before going to sleep. I can honestly say that in the seven plus years we shared together, we never went to bed angry with each other, we also always said "I Love You" before going to sleep. It helps to know someone really cares and that you're not alone.

E. DO read the tabloids, those market scandal sheets - You never know what good information you'll find on the subject of sex and romance. Some of its just trash but I have gotten some very worthwhile information from them over the years.

F. DO keep an open mind - When it comes to maintaining a good relationship, you can never learn enough. Share your information with your companion; it might be just what you need. If it's something funny, you'll both get a good laugh out of it and a good laugh, together, will stimulate your sexual desire.

LIST YOUR OWN DOs HERE:

**THIS PAGE IS FOR YOU TO
ADD YOUR OWN DO's.**

4. The CAN Dos

The CAN DOs are a little different from the DOs. The CAN DOs are optional; you can do them if you want to. They are some small or inexpensive things you can do to keep the romance alive in your relationship.

A. Have a movie night at home - Put in a movie, turn off the lights, and cozy up on the couch with popcorn and sodas.
B. Go out for a drive - Park and sit to look at city lights or star gaze.
C. Each of you make a list of the positive things about your relationship and the things you like about each other - Read them together over a wine and cheese snack.
D. Plan to have a night out - dinner and a movie work well. Pie and coffee is also good.
E. Share a bath or shower together - Wash each other. Enjoy being together without the sexual encounter.
F. Recreate your first meeting or your first date - It might rekindle some forgotten feelings. My husband, J.B., liked going to a coffee shop. We'd drive in separately, I'd go in first, and then he'd come in and pretend that he was picking me up. He said that it made him feel younger to be able to pickup a pretty 'young chick'.
G. Go window-shopping together - Don't buy, just look. Look at things that you both like. It will give you a chance to dream together.

H. Buy him a small gift - A key chain or copper bracelet is good. (Copper promotes good health.)

I. Give him a friendship card - This is a good idea, especially, if you can't find the words to tell him how much you care. Put in a handwritten note, an I.O.U. for a back rub, foot rub, night out or romantic night in, or breakfast in bed. Be creative.

J. Spring for a box of chocolates - Good chocolate may have an ingredient (phenylethylalanine) found in cocoa that affects the pleasure center in the brain.

K. Plan an evening together - just the two of you with no interruptions. Unplug the telephone if you have to. (For more information, see Special Events.)

L. Give him flowers - Many men appreciate flowers almost as much as women do. A single rose will say thank you while a complete bouquet may have many meanings. Be sure to attach a card so the meanings are correctly understood.

Just Flowers?

My husband, Tom, is always apologizing for his love of flowers. Somehow, he's been convinced that it's not a manly thing. Many florists are men and so are the growers and nursery people. My grandfather was a past President of the Pasadena Rose Society. Flowers can say so much from the thank you (gratitude) of a single rose to the fabled remembrance of the Rosemary. If you'd rather do a plant that lasts, than a bouquet that fades, give a Chrysanthemum plant. Chrysanthemum represents love and the plant, when rooted, will produce blooms for a long time.

The history of flower language goes back to 17th Century Turkey. Flowers, along with other items such as feathers, string, and stones, were used to send coded messages, understood only by the sender and the receiver. In 1718, the Lady Mary Wortley, wife of the British Ambassador to Constantinople, wrote home about the secret language of flowers. In 1819, Madame Charlotte de la Tour (pen name for Louise Cortambert) wrote and published a dictionary, on the meaning of flowers, entitled <u>Le Language des Fleurs</u>. During the Victorian Era, in England, it was popular for lovers to send bouquets, called Tussie-Mussies, to convey feelings they were unable to display openly. In 1884, London, a book was published by Jean Marsh, illustrated by Kate Greenaway, entitled <u>the Language of Flowers</u>.

I have found several lists, of flowers with their meanings, some for European flowers and some flowers common to only the eastern United States. I have tried to list those that I feel are pretty common everywhere and fairly easy to obtain at your local florist.

Flower	Meaning
Aster	Symbol of love
Basil	Best wishes
Borage	Courage
Broom	Humility
Carnation (pink)	I'll never forget you
Carnation (red)	My heart aches for you
Carnation (striped)	Refusal
China Rose	My poor heart aches for you
Chrysanthemum	Love
Coreopsis	Love at first sight
Daffodil	Regards
Daisy	Innocence, newborn
Forget-Me-Nots	True love

Flower	Meaning
Gardenia	Ecstasy
Geranium	You are childish
Heather	Admiration
Hyacinth	I'm sorry, forgive me
Ivy	Fidelity friendship, and marriage
Jasmine	Grace
Lavender	Luck, devotion
Lilac	First Love
Lily	Purity, modesty
Lily of the Valley	Purity, return of happiness
Marigold	Health, grief, despair
Marjoram	Kindness, courtesy
Orchid	Love, beauty, refinement
Pansy	Loving thoughts
Periwinkle	Happy memory
Primrose	I can't live without you
Rose (cabbage)	Ambassador of love
Rose (pink)	Grace, beauty
Rose (red)	Love, passionate love
Rose (white)	Innocence, purity, silence and spiritual love
Rose (yellow)	Friendship, jealousy
Flower	Meaning
Rosemary	Remembrance
Sage	Gratitude
Sweet Pea	Tender memory
Sweet William	Gallantry
Tulip (red)	My perfect lover and reclamation of love
Violet	Loyalty, modesty, humility

Violet (blue)	Faithfulness
Wallflower	Fidelity

The giving of multiple roses, any color, also has meanings:

1 rose	Gratitude, simplicity
2 roses	Mutual feelings
3 roses	I love you
10 roses	You are perfect
12 roses	Be mine
13 roses	Friends forever
15 roses	I'm truly sorry
24 roses	Forever yours
25 roses	Congratulations
50 roses	Unconditional love
99 roses	I'll love you all the days of my life
108 roses	Will you marry me?
999 roses (a roomful)	I'll love you till the end of time

You can find a more detailed list, and history, at: www.kansascuties.com/articles/the-language-and-meaning-of-flowers.shtml.

Remember to enclose, or attach, a card so your true meanings are understood. Choose the flowers, or floral bouquet, yourself or with the advice of a knowledgeable florist. Flowers are also the plants' way of saying thank you for taking care of them.

Judith Morland

Love, as a partially opened flower is,

in its beginning,

frustrating and painful.

It's only when in full bloom that we can

realize the full potential of Love's

fulfillment and satisfaction.

-JMC 9/21/1990

- YOUR PERSONAL NOTES HERE -

5. Special Events

Imagine, once more, your road journey. The CAN Dos would have been the viewpoints, the short pleasant stops. Now we go on to the scenic routes, the longer more enjoyable times you can share with your companion. These are the special events. They may take a little planning but when done properly and with patience, they should prove to be most enjoyable for both of you.

A.   A Night of Romance

These are just some suggestions. You may want to use only two or three of them at a time OR do them all at once. To get the most out of them, unplug your telephone, to prevent interruptions AND if you have children, find an over night babysitter: 1. Dress sexily; 2. Share a beverage and/or a snack; 3. Share a bath; 4. A massage, or foot rub (or both); 5. The sexual encounter. Sound easy? Read the descriptions:

1. Dress sexily - When I was a teenager, my mother read an article that suggested to surprise your husband, wrap yourself in plastic food wrap and meet him at the door. I think that's over doing it a bit but it might be worth a try. Be sure he doesn't have a friend with him, it could be very embarrassing. The idea is to dress in what he thinks is sexy. The same thing could be done with a fur (faux, of course) coat and little, if anything underneath. If he likes the French Maid costume, go with that.

2. Share a beverage or snack - For an evening of romance you want to serve a sexually stimulating beverage. For something warm and simple try Lipton® tea steeped with lemon, cinnamon, ginger, honey or peppermint. Brew the tea first then add the flavoring. Use honey to sweeten. A nice tea is an orange tea with cinnamon and sweetened to taste with honey. If you don't want to do tea, you can use hot orange juice with cinnamon and honey. Apple juice flavored with cinnamon also is nice. If it's cold outside, try hot chocolate with a little cinnamon. If your companion has no problems with high blood pressure, you can offer him tea with ginseng in it. Try one of the following:

Beverage Recipes

Spiced Tea[5] (best served hot)
1/2 Cup of water
3/4 Cup of sugar

Bring to boil then add:

1/4 Cup of orange juice
1/2 Cup of lemon juice
6 cloves
1 cinnamon stick

Add to regular brewed tea - 2 bags per pot.

Ginger Tea[6] (best served hot)
3" piece of ginger, thinly sliced   juice of 2 lemons
1 Cup of mint leaves   6 Cups of water
6 tea bags (green tea is best)
1/2 Cup honey

Add ginger to water - bring to boil - remove from heat - Add mint and tea bags - steep 30mins. - Strain into pitcher - Add honey and lemon - Serve hot in mugs OR may be chilled and served over ice.

Mint tea[7] (best served chilled)
1/2 Cup chilled tonic water
1/2 teaspoon sugar crushed ice (best) cubes otherwise
1/2 teaspoon lemon juice or 1/2 teaspoon lime juice
2 tablespoons grapefruit juice
4 sprigs of mint

Blend together all but mint. Add mint last and garnish glasses with a lemon slice. Sweeten if desired.

Milk Cooler (My grandmother's recipe)
4 Cups cold milk
12 tablespoons canned strained peaches
4 tablespoons honey
1/4 teaspoon cinnamon

Blend together and chill. May add ice, if desired.

Apple juice warm up
3 Cups apple juice
1/4 teaspoon cinnamon, ginger or allspice - Serve hot in mugs.

Snacks, or light meal, can follow the beverage of choice. A good snack would be a vegetable tray with raw broccoli, cauliflower, and celery sticks. Broccoli and cauliflower contain sulfur that provides pep for romance. Celery provides sodium, which neutralizes acids, helps digestion, and makes you feel ready for love. Strawberries and chocolate (for dipping) are also a good sex snack. Good chocolate has a natural chemical in it that can arouse the pleasure center of the brain. Strawberries, with their heart like shape, have been long associated with romance. If strawberries won't work (some people are allergic to them) try bananas. Bananas dip well in chocolate and provide potassium, needed for hormone production and to insure healthy nerves and muscles. If you're adventurous, and don't mind baking, try the sex or power muffins. To bake these take one of the muffin recipes provided and add 6 capsules of ginseng (for sex) or ginkgo biloba (for power) and, add 1 teaspoon of ginger or cinnamon and orange rinds for flavoring. Be careful with the ginseng although it's used a lot nowadays, a little goes a long way and it can cause problems in those with high blood pressure. There are no known side effects with ginkgo biloba, so you could use up to 10 capsules if desired. Ginkgo biloba will give a nice feeling of well being. If you wish to dress the muffins up further, you can add semi sweet chocolate bits to the mix, or 2 ounces of melted chocolate (melt it with 1 tablespoon butter then add to mix).

Muffin Mixes[8]

Standard Muffin Mix (makes about 20 muffins)
1 3/4 Cup all purpose flour
2 eggs
3/4 teaspoon salt
3 tablespoons melted butter
1/4 Cup sugar (or 1/3 Cup of honey)
3/4 Cup milk (if too dry add 1/4 Cup more)
2 teaspoons double acting baking powder

Beat eggs - add milk and butter - Sift dry ingredients together Mix egg mix into flour mixture. Bake at 400°F. 20-25 mins. in greased, or Pam® sprayed, muffin pan.

Whole Grain Muffins
1 1/2 cups whole grain flour
2 tablespoons molasses
1 teaspoon salt
2 teaspoons baking powder
1 egg
1 cup milk
3 teaspoons melted butter
1 - 2 tablespoons grated orange rind

Combine dry ingredients - Beat egg then combine with milk and butter - mix into flour mixture - add orange rind. Pour into greased muffin pan. Bake at 400° F. for 20-25 mins.

Berry Muffins
Use Standard Muffin Mix but add:
1/3 cup sugar
1/4 cup melted butter
1 cup blueberries
1 cup cranberries
1 teaspoon grated orange or lemon rind

Standard Bran Muffins
2 cups all purpose or whole grain flour
1 1/2 cup bran
2 tablespoons sugar
1/4 Teaspoon salt
1 1/4 teaspoon baking soda
2 cups buttermilk
1 egg
1/2 cup molasses
3 tablespoons melted butter

Mix dry ingredients in large bowl - Beat buttermilk, eggs, molasses and melted butter together then combine with dry mixture - Pour into greased muffin pan - Bake at 400° F. for 25 mins.

Fancy Snack Bread (OK to add
some ginkgo biloba here)

Rosemary Bread[9]
1 package yeast (1/4 ounce)
1 1/2 cups whole wheat flour
1 1/2 cups self rising flour
2 tablespoons butter or margarine
1/4 cup warm water
1 cup whole milk (2% milk is OK)
1 tablespoon sugar
1 teaspoon salt
1 tablespoon sesame seeds (optional)
1 tablespoon dried chopped onions (good but optional)
1 tablespoon fresh rosemary leaves (add more to decorate)
1 cup cubed cheddar cheese (best, but can use American cheese)
Coarse salt (for decoration)

Mix yeast with flour, sift together into bowl. Melt butter. To flour mix, stir in melted butter, water, milk, sugar, salt, sesame seeds, onions, cheese, and rosemary. Knead thoroughly until smooth. Place dough in a clean greased bowl, turn so all sides are greased. Cover with a clean dry cloth and allow 1 1/2 hours to rise in a dry place. Place dough in a greased 9" X 5" loaf pan and press into loaf form. Recover and let rise another 1 hour longer. Bake at 375° F. for 30 mins. The last 5-10 mins.

cover with foil to prevent burning. Remove from pan to wire rack for cooling. Decorate top with rosemary leaves and coarse salt. Enjoy.

3. Share a bath - There is nothing like soaking in a lavender, or rose, scented bath to get things going. A shower with lavender bath gel is good too, but quicker. This is your night to enjoy yourselves so take your time. Wash each other and play with the soap foam. Be sure to get 'squeaky' clean.

4. A massage or foot rub - Set the mood first, turn down the bed, dim the lights and scent the room. If you have a bedside light put in a pink light bulb (pink is one of the colors associated with romance). A rose scented candle or patchouli incense (patchouli is reputed to arouse sexual interest) will complete the mood. Have your companion lie down for a massage. Of course, you can skip the massage and go right into the sexual encounter but why rush it. This is a night for romance and massage is a form of sensual touching. There are many forms of massage to choose from but I'll tell you about aural, chakra and standard massage. Aural and chakra massage can be performed on either the front or the back of the body, and best done without body oil. For a night of romance, begin with your companion lying on his back.

Aural massage is a unique form of massage without actually touching. The aura is our life force emanating within us. It is so strong that it forms a frame around our physical body. Although some people can actually see it, most people feel it as a warm sensation. Take your hands, palms down, position them side by side but with one slightly in front of the other. Move them slowly up and down your companion's body. Try to stay about a quarter inch above him. Pay particular notice to any areas that feel different, usually cooler or tingly. Go over your companion slowly and thoroughly. Then lower your hands to touch him. End at the head or shoulders, wherever you plan to start the next form of massage.

The next form of massage is called chakra massage. When I was a child, my grandmother used it on me. If I had a headache, or stomachache, she'd have me lie down on the couch and she'd gently press, with her warm hands, where I was sore. It also calmed me. She was using chakra massage. Chakra is a Sanskrit word meaning "wheel" of energy. Imagine little wheels of energy spinning in different, but major, parts of your body. As long as they spin freely our body functions normally. When they become blocked, or sluggish, we have physical health problems. There are chakras throughout the body but with simple chakra massage you only touch the seven major ones: 1. the crown; 2. the third eye; 3. the throat; 4. the heart; 5. the solar plexus; 6. the sacral; 7. the base chakras. Beginning at the top: the crown chakra brings together the connection of the mind, spirit and body; the third eye chakra is your sense of awareness and intuitive self; the throat chakra is linked with your ability to speak the truth (it's also the location of your thyroid gland); the heart chakra is your emotions, love and joy; the solar plexus chakra is your center of empowerment; the sacral chakra is your awareness of abundance sensuality and sexuality; the base chakra your issues of survival and security. Locate each chakra in the following manner and lay your warm hands on each area as you move slowly down the list. Touch gently so your companion can feel the warmth from your hands. As you get into this, you may feel the warmth flowing through you and into your companion.

1. The crown chakra - found on the top of the head, as if your companion is wearing a crown. Place your warm hands on the top of your companion's head. It's not necessary to press here, especially if they have a headache, but hold to the count of five.
2. The third eye chakra (also known as the brow chakra) – Place both hands on the face, palms on the cheekbones and fingertips on the brow. Leave a nose space. Press gently and hold to the count of five.
3. The throat chakra - Place your hands lightly around the throat, heels of the palms touching in front and fingers wrapping toward the back. It is not necessary to wrap all the way around. Hold only to the count of three. This warmth should also help the thyroid gland.
4. The heart chakra - Place your hands on the chest area just above each breast. Press lightly and hold to the count of five.
5. The solar plexus chakra - Place your hands on the chest area just below each breast, feel the stomach muscle. Press lightly and hold to the count of five.
6. The sacral chakra - Place your hands just above the waist line, fingertips pointing in. Press lightly and hold to the count of five.
7. The base chakra - Place your hands over the lower abdomen with fingers pointing down toward the genital region. Press very gently, but don't tickle. Hold to the count of three. Chakra massage can also be used along with your normal maintenance massage. There are also corresponding chakras up the back area that you may stimulate during normal

massage. Now, have your companion rollover and lie face down for the next massage.

The romantic standard massage - Begin with your companion lying face down on the bed and sit along side of him. Gently rub your companion's neck and shoulders first. Use a gentle kneading motion on the shoulders. Rub a few minutes then take a break to apply some barely warm body oil. Be careful to use only a little, too much gets too messy later. You can purchase ready- made massage oil, even a warming one. You can also use baby oil or mineral oil. Add 3 drops each of rosemary oil and lavender oil to 1/2 cup baby, or mineral, oil. Rosemary and lavender are known as muscle relaxers and body soothers. Rub his back slowly and evenly, moving lower as you progress. Take your time with his lower back area, there is a sensitive spot, which may arouse him. Be sure you rub his thighs and calves before reaching his feet. The points on the foot to stimulate sexual desire would be on the sale just in front of the heel and also on the edge of the inner side, just above the bend, of each foot. The area on the sole of the foot reflects the sacral area of the body. It connects with our awareness of abundance, sensuality, and sexuality. The area on the inside edge of the foot corresponds with the testes, need I say more. Have your companion turn over on his back and gently rub the top of his feet, calves, thighs then look at him and smile, he'll let you know what comes next.

5. The sexual encounter - At this point I don't feel it's necessary for me to describe the actual love making techniques. I've set the stage for you - you do the acting. If you need advice read some of Ann Hooper's books on sex OR even older books by

Xaviera Hollander (aka the Happy Hooker). See the Suggested Reading list. If you have plenty of time, you may want to choose some sex play listed in the next section, Sex, Fun and Games.

B.   Sex, Fun and Games

In our world, with specific interest to mammals, there are two types of sex. Type one, is basic Biology 101, sex for reproduction. Type two, bearing on human behavior, is sexual contact for pleasure, enjoyment, fulfillment as well as reproduction. I'd like to say that type two is entirely a human experience but I have some doubts with the behavior of dogs and monkeys.

Basic reproduction sex is sexual contact, penetration, by mammals to perpetuate their species. Although, there are usually noises, grunts and groans, involved, there is, according to science, no particular enjoyment factor, particularly for the female. Chickens display this rather interestingly. The rooster comes up to a hen, who is scratching and pecking the ground, jumps on her, for all of the count of four, hops off, crows very loudly and parades around the yard. The hen merely straightens up, fluffs her feathers, and goes back to scratching and pecking. The female obviously gets no enjoyment. There is a certain amount of foreplay with some mammals. Male goats (bucks and billys) will take time to 'perfume' themselves, rub up against their chosen female (doe), lick her sides, make strange gobbling sounds, then jump on her. The doe just stands there and when it's done goes back to whatever she was doing. Again, the female has no enjoyment.

Sexual contact with humans is a different story altogether. There are some religions that shun the enjoyment part in favor of the sex for reproduction, perpetuation of the species, only. In other words, a man can only have sexual contact, penetration, with his wife when they are intending to produce children. The use of contraception devices was also frowned upon. Perpetuation of the species is a good thing but there are an awful lot of people in this world already. If God didn't intend for us to enjoy sex why did He give us the urges, desires, and feelings? Surely, He intended for us to experience the sharing of such a wonderful contact with our Chosen Companion. However, when you have sexual contact without children in mind, please protect yourself with some type of contraception. Be very careful not to acquire a sexually transmitted disease, including AIDS. You may trust your companion now but you don't really know about their past contacts.

God gave human beings the special ability to enjoy the sexual encounter in ways unlike any other mammal. Although it does not state it in the Bible, I believe that God may have given this special ability to the female to compensate her for the pain of childbirth. Sexual contact, for the female, is much more than reproduction or physical release (as it is for the male) it involves emotional and mental satisfaction for total fulfillment. When male and female work at it together, they can achieve immeasurable heights of passion and enjoyment. Thus, there are three main levels of sexual contact that can be experienced. It is your duty, as the female, to help your male reach the desired level.

Level 1

The standard 'quickie', on-and-off, 'wham, bam, thank you mam', type of sex. This is usually a time of physical release for the male with no particular interest given to the female's desires. This level is mainly a 'body thing'. Man is, basically, a selfish individual.

When he feels the need, for physical release, he wants it now. It is your duty as his caregiver, to take care of his need. If you are unable to do so often enough, he may 'seek another barnyard to scratch in'. If you're lucky, he'll take a cold shower, or 'take it in hand' and wait for another time with you. Many men never leave this level of sex. It is your duty to take him by the hand and lead him onto Level 2.

Level 2

Is the broadest of the three levels. This is the level of discovery and experimentation, where the fun and games happen and the male develops some actual concern for the needs of the female. The male suddenly realizes that he gets more satisfaction if he spends a little effort concentrating on the feelings, physical and emotional, of his companion. This newfound consideration, by the male, opens up a whole world of sexual enjoyment for both companions. Many men may find that, although they have a hard time expressing themselves verbally to their companion, now they can express themselves through their loving actions. A very rough, calloused, coarse looking man may turn out to be the most tender and affectionate lover.

The most important thing about Level 2 is that you shouldn't begin unless you both desire to. If one companion doesn't feel quite up to par the performance, on both parts, will be off and the experience will not be good. It may be better, at that time to fall back to Level 1 and save Level 2 for another time.

When you are both ready let the games begin. Level 2 is a time for discovering each other and experimenting with sensations. Through different 'games' from touching, using devices, to actual role-playing you learn how to please each other. By stimulation of the physical body and the mind you will enhance your senses (sight, smell, hearing, taste and feeling) and increase your physical and mental awareness. Where Level I was more related to a body need, Level 2 now involves both the body and the mind.

Each 'game' will develop a sense, listed. The Touch and Tease and actual role-playing games involve complete trust in your companion. Trust yourselves to do no harm to each other. If something becomes physically or emotionally uncomfortable, it should be discontinued at once. The following is a list of some 'games' you might want to try. Start slowly and work toward the more complicated games:

Sense of Time:

The Afternoon Delight - also known as 'a nooner'. If you normally perform love making at night, a daytime session might be a pleasant change.

Sense of Environment:

The Great Outdoors - Be sure to choose an isolated spot so you're not interrupted. This can be done day or night. If you're fortunate, you might locate a stream, or lake, or at least a nice patch of grass and a tree. I have a friend who enjoyed the warm hood of a car with, or without, the engine running.

Theme rooms - In the more populated cities some motels are featuring theme rooms. Themes include: a forest room, complete with a babbling brook; a sultan's den; a jungle; and an island retreat. You can experience the outdoors indoors.

In-Home Surface Sex - Perform love making on different surfaces, other than your bed. Surfaces might include: a soft carpet; a chair or couch; standing against a wall; over a bar stool; a table; bathroom counter; and the shower or bathtub. Use your imagination.

Sense of Smell:

Petal Power - Set up your room with the sensation of roses. Put in a pink light bulb, light a rose scented candle and spread rose petals on the bed. My oldest daughter suggests white or pink petals as the dark red petals will stain the sheets.

Sense of Hearing:

Music - Vary the music you choose to make love by. Instead of mood music, try classical or jazz. You can also obtain a light that keeps beat with the music.

Sense of Taste:

Whipped Cream - now it comes in chocolate. A can of Reddiwip® is always handy for fun. You can put it on him in spots that he would enjoy having it licked off. You can also appear, from the bathroom, dressed in a whipped cream bikini and he can do the licking.

Flavored Oils - There are oils available flavored with chocolate, peppermint or fruit flavors, also cinnamon. My oldest daughter warns that they may not taste as expected, and that they can get sticky, so expect to shower off, but they may still be worth the trouble.

Sense of Sight:

Some men get very turned on by their lady being partially dressed in 'something lacey', a teddy, garter belt, and stockings, then they like being 'out of sight', (looking around a corner), as she slowly removes them. There are those who like to watch the strip tease right in front of them. Then there are those who want to watch a whole private sexual encounter (masturbation) and then suddenly come in to help finish. To do this you not only have to trust your companion, you have to have some hefty self-confidence, and self esteem.

Sense of Touch (feel):

Body Paints - These are fun. You get to feel the paint as you draw on each other. Make sure you get the ones for sex games. Draw hearts, arrows, stars, and bulls-eyes on each other. You can even draw breasts on him and a penis on yourself. It all washes off in the shower.

The Feel of Oil - Use lots of it. This is best done with a rubber sheet; or a shower curtain. The idea is to oil each other up and have a slippery good time. Do this on the floor so you don't slip off the bed.

Touch and Tease - For this you need a box with different objects in it. Select things that feel different, for example; a feather, a soft cloth, sand paper, a sponge, a fork, a rolling pin, a flower and a soft brush. You will also need a small hand held, battery operated vibrator AND a blindfold. You can use a scarf but the idea is no peeking. This game will help build trust. Have your companion lie naked on the bed, blindfold him, take each item, not in any particular order, and gently stroke him with it. Ask him to identify it. To finish this game, take the vibrator and tease his sensitive spots. This game can be performed by both companions. There are numerous styles and shapes of vibrators available but choose one simple model that you both can enjoy.

Role Games (Mind Play):

Some role games involve costumes so look for costumes around Halloween, unless you're a seamstress with imagination. The importance of role games is that they stimulate the mind. You are not just yourself you are an actress/actor, and you must both play your part. It is important, when playing role games, that you have a special word to let you out if the going gets too rough. Once this word is said, everything stops. Choose a word unrelated, and make sure it's understood by both of you.

It's best if you make up your own games as you go along but some themes might be: doctor and nurse; man cop and lady victim; lady cop and man victim; hooker and John and the patient and the candy striper. There's always the French Maid who has to do what Simon Says. Use your imagination.

The last two games involve complete trust in each other. Play Rape - the woman dresses in an old dress, one that she doesn't mind if it gets torn, and the man comes in and has his way with her. The man should not perform anything that you're not used to doing, normally, unless it's been previously agreed to at the choice of the game. Mutual Masturbation - You must have a lot of self-esteem and self-confidence to do this. The idea is to stimulate each other by sight, touching your own self only, and see who comes to climax first. Sharing this experience is difficult because even though you're both there you can't touch each other until it's over. It is best not to dwell on these last two games too much. The sexual encounter is meant to be a beautiful union between caring companions. It should not be allowed to become something hurtful, harmful, or kinky and dirty.

Remember the use of sex games is to enhance the senses, physical and mental, and build trust in each other. By sharing these sensations with your chosen companion, you will develop deeper feelings of trust and respectful love for each other. Spend lots of time on Level 2, and learn about your companion and yourself. When you fully understand, or at least you think that you do your companion's physical needs and emotional desires it's time to move on to Level 3. Some companions prefer to remain on Level 2, but if you want to go on you should not cheat yourselves of the experience.

Level 3

Level 3 is the one of mutual respect and admiration. You are both open and honest and are no longer sexually inhibited. There is no need now for games and role-playing. You are now above all of that. Your lovemaking becomes more intense with consideration of both companions. You are now also more emotionally aware of each other. Your primary thought is to please your companion completely, physically, mentally and now spiritually. It is harder for men to display their emotions openly so you must assure him that it's all right to do so. It is when you are communicating, sexually, on an emotion to emotion basis, that you will be able to feel your souls touch.

Level 3 is the highest level that the sexual encounter can take you. Many older religions, cults, and lifestyles, with teachings going back much further than the advent of Christianity, believe that man and woman can feel the closest to God when they experience climax together. This is called the feeling of Oneness, two souls reaching out and touching each other for spiritual enlightenment, soul growth. It is believed that they actually get a glimpse of heaven. It takes patience, understanding, and deep respectful love, of each other, to achieve this. It is also done with a pure heart. There is almost no way to describe this feeling without having felt it. It is the uniting of two souls, two minds, and two bodies. With this feeling of Oneness, you become not only spiritually aware of each other but of the peace and harmony in the world around you. You realize how wonderful the gift of life is, and in doing so, you'll find your nitch in life's scheme of things.

The master philosophers believed that through knowledge and meditation, combined with discipline, clean living, they could attain this level without the sexual encounter. They gave up their material needs and concentrated only on the needs of the mind and soul. They are the masters, our spiritual teachers, leading us on the path toward oneness with God, our creator. They are the gifted ones with higher enlightenment but they do deprive themselves of the feeling of Oneness shared by two loving companions.

As an American Geisha, you are required to fulfill your companion's sexual needs on all levels. You will also need to keep the experiences varied to hold your companion's interest.

The Kama Sutra

Somewhere between 100 and 500 A.D. there lived, in India, a scholar named Vatsyayana. He took the wisdom of his sages, the master scholars and philosophers of his time, added his observations of his own countrymen, and compiled a work entitled the Kama Sutra. The main purpose of the Kama Sutra was to instruct a male citizen on everyday life. It included instructions of everything from one's grooming habits, which at that time included perfuming himself and staining his teeth red or black, to how he should occupy his time and even to his sexual habits and appetites. It not only told the man who he could have sex with but how to do it. It also informed him how to choose a suitable wife, and how she should be trained.

What we, as modern day Americans, have borrowed from this ancient text is the use of positions so that the man, and woman, could experience a heightened emotional and pleasurable level of sex. Many of the positions suggested in the Kama Sutra have to do with lifting and repositioning the legs. A simple example of this would be, for you and your companion to: begin in the missionary position, lying face to face man on top legs stretched out; slowly raise your knees while keeping your feet flat until your knees are completely bent upwards; open your thighs by moving your knees outward; slowly lift your lower legs until you form an open V-shape; then wrap your legs around your companion's waist. You have now completed five positions in one fairly smooth and flowing motion.

To try something a little more advanced, return your legs to the missionary position; both of you turn on your side without disengaging from your companion; wrap your top leg around your companion's waist; have your companion move his leg underneath you and roll up into a sitting position facing each other and finally embrace. There are many more positions mentioned in the Kama Sutra, some more advanced, as moving your legs on up to bend against your, and his, chest and hooking them over his shoulders, also, entry from the back and more embracing positions. If you're really interested in the other positions, you need a good book for further instruction. Please see list in Suggested Reading. The positions were suggested for deeper penetration, by the man, and increased friction, for the woman, for ultimate mutual enjoyment and spiritual fulfillment.

The Tantra and Tantric Sex

As with the positions of the Kama Sutra, the practice of Tantric Sex also teaches reaching spiritual enlightenment through heightened, passionate, and emotional sex. However rather than dealing with it on a physical level, tantric sex approaches the same goal, spiritual fulfillment, dealing more with the mind, and the sexual connection, of the companions.

The actual practice of Tantra is of a very religious nature and is an entire way of living. It goes into the deep beliefs of the Hindus, the Buddhists, and the Taoists. To properly practice the beliefs of Tantra you need to have a guru, a master teacher, to guide you. What we have borrowed from the tantric beliefs is the aspect of harnessing the energies of the body, the emotions of the mind, with sexual energy as a means to the ultimate goal of attaining spiritual enlightenment and realization of the true nature of reality. With respect to being an American Geisha, you must be able to understand some simple basics of Tantra and to love your companion wholly and completely, with every cell in your body.

Tantra, its teachings and beliefs, is the basis for most of the world's oldest religions. Actually, rather than just a religion, Tantra is a whole way of living. The symbolic drawings of Tantra, known as yantra, decorate the oldest ruins ever found. They are seen on the walls of temples and pyramids of the Middle and Far East to the temples of the Mayan and Aztec Indians as well as on the pottery and fabrics of our own North American Indians. These symbols were around long before we had the written word. The doctrine of Tantra teaches that life began as a Cosmic Egg from which hatched the universe, heaven and earth. The Hindus believe the Lord Shiva, the creator, came out of a lotus plant, with his female consort, the goddess Shakti. They further believe, that our manifested universe was caused by the union of Lord Shiva and goddess Shakti. Shiva is considered as the mighty creator (our God) and Shakti is the essence of energy (the Light). The pair may be depicted in paintings sitting inside a lotus blossom. The practice of Tantra involves balancing the opposing qualities of the female and the male. Tantra also proposes that there is a divine being in each of us, a god (male) or a goddess (female). This thought refers to the energy, creative force and cosmic power within us. The goddess is honored for her feminine qualities, of lover, seductress, healer, nurturing mother, while the god is honored for the male qualities, of provider, protector, power symbol, nurturing and healing. The art of Tantric Sex salutes the god and goddess in each of us and celebrates, with our union, the union of Shiva (whose energy is also known as bliss) and Shakti (whose energy is also known as knowledge). In other words, the joining of bliss and knowledge results in spiritual enlightenment.

To experience a simple form of Tantric Sex you need to apply the principles of meditation and knowledge of the body's chakras, with your sexual union. As with most sexual encounters, you will need to be 'squeaky' clean, including your breath, before you begin. It's nice if you share a bath and wash each other before doing this exercise. With reference to the body chakras, for the purpose of Tantric Sex, you begin at the spine, the base chakra and move upward to the crown chakra.

A Taste of Tantric Sex - Sit astride your companion, female on top, with your legs wrapped around his hips. This sitting position should align both your chakras. Connect yourselves sexually. Close your eyes and meditate. The tantrics may use either a mantra (a single sound or a chant) or a yantra (a visualized symbol) to focus on. You should focus on the triangle, which also happens to be a yantra. You, as the female, should imagine yourself as the inverted triangle, with the point as your female genitals (the yoni). Your companion should imagine himself as the upright triangle, the point representing his penis (the lingam). Begin to take alternate breaths with your companion. As you breathe in imagine drawing your breath up from your yoni, through your body and out into your companion. Your companion then breathes in your breath, draws it through his body and out his lingam, which has been inserted into your yoni, and the cycle begins again. It becomes a circle of connected breaths. Continue to do this as long as possible. As the sexual energy builds between you imagine your energy as a snake coiled beneath your spine. Wake up this sleeping snake (the kundalini) and draw it up through each of your body chakras, pausing long enough to feel the sensations from each chakra. Pulling up your energy together will increase these sensations. While you're drawing up your energy, picture the joining of the two triangles to form the six-pointed star, the divine couple. End with the last chakra, the crown, for your energy to join together in exaltation of your union. This should be a unique experience even for beginners. For more information on the Practice of Tantric Sex please see Suggested Reading.

So now, you've traveled down your road together. You've managed to avoid most of the potholes and you have checked out all three levels. Where to go now? Well, once you've made it to the top you can always go back down a level or two, when necessary, and enjoy just being together. Save the experience of Level 3 for those special times when you have the time, and take your time to enjoy each other.

6. The Rewards

"He who finds a wife finds a good thing,
and obtains favor from the Lord."

In the days of Vatsyayana, a woman was trained in numerous things. She was required to know the arts of: singing, dancing, playing musical instruments, writing, drawing, adorning an idol, gardening, staining and dyeing of fabrics, teeth, hair, nails and bodies, fixing stained glass in a floor, making beds, spreading out carpets, playing music on glasses filled with water, picture making and decorating, stringing necklaces, making garlands, preparing perfumes, proper adornment with jewelry, magic or sorcery, cooking, making lemonades and sherbets, sewing, reading, carpentry, architecture, chemistry, mineralogy, mines and quarries, making artificial flowers, poetry, pottery and, of course, how to entertain a man. In the copy of the Kama Sutra that I read there was a page and a half of listed things that a woman had to know. Even with all this knowledge, if she didn't satisfy her husband in any way, he was permitted to obtain a second wife. There was no such thing as divorce, the man just added more wives. The wives shared the duties but they had to compete for the love of their husband.

In our time, women can learn things as they go along. What we don't learn from our parents, or in school, we can learn through experiences. The key is to keep an open mind, try to learn something new everyday. Give your all to your relationship with your chosen companion, be it sex or just great conversation. What will you receive for all your trouble? Besides a great time in the sack, somewhere along the road you'll find the gift of unconditional love. Unconditional love is one of the most precious rewards love has to offer. It comes as the relationship matures, usually over years. You love your companion, not in spite of their flaws but because of them. You may not always like what they do but you love them anyway. Once it's felt by both of you, there is nothing else like it. This is the stuff that cements everything, the stuff that lovers die for, and the best thing is that if it doesn't come naturally it can be learned with patience and understanding. It is a real reward.

This gift is given to do with what you may.

I hope you'll be gracious and not make me pay.

To give this gift it cost me much,

Pettiness, jealousy, inconsideration and such.

It is given with hope that it will be returned.

Also to be kept, to cherish and to be burned.

The best place to keep it is close to your heart.

To have it, to hold it to keep it a part.

It is not expensive but valued beyond measure.

It is given for free, for you to treasure.

It has no restrictions, it knows no bounds.

It is given by many, the whole world round.

Created for woman to give to her man.

Given to her by God's holy hand.

This special gift from God up above -

The gift I give you, Unconditional Love.

-JMC 11/30/91

CONCLUSION

With life, there is a reason, a purpose. Our purpose in life, other than to perpetuate our species, is to experience soul growth, so that we may attain our highest level of enlightenment and ultimately become one with God. For most of us, soul growth is achieved by first becoming aware of your self, then reaching out to others, and finally making the perfect connection, a complete union with another soul. Not everyone has the natural gift of the masters, but we can have the enjoyment of the road to achieve the same end. Your duty, as an American Geisha, is to raise your family and help your Chosen Companion reach his desired level of enlightenment. In doing so, you will also achieve your own chosen level.

What happens when we grow old? Well, those of us who've had experiences can teach those open and willing to learn. Just remember that it's never too late for love. I just recently found out that my mother has a new boyfriend. He holds her hand and whispers sweet nothings in her ear. She says that he's very attentive. She's just like a giddy schoolgirl with her first crush. He's 89 years old, and my mother...is 91 years young. It's also never too late to achieve your own personal goals. Do not be discouraged. If one relationship fails, there's always a chance of finding another one and you will be stronger and wiser the next time. Be true to yourself, always do the best you can and you will not only enjoy life - life will enjoy you.

When I originally put together the first draft of American Geisha, in 1991, it was more a series of random thoughts. I had recently had a near death experience and I was afraid that I wouldn't have time to convey my thoughts to my youngest daughter, who at that time was five years old. My oldest daughter was already grown, and married, and I had not given any thought about American Geisha being of use to her. As it turned out, American Geisha can be of help to any woman at any time she finds herself without a companion or just wants some idea of what to do with the one she has. American Geisha is more than just a guidebook, it's a celebration of life's shared experiences. Although mostly inspired writing, there was a lot of back up research done. Take what you want of my thoughts, rearrange them to suit your own personal needs and use them to not only guide you but enrich your life as well. If you have good experiences, you'll have many wonderful memories you can pass on. When it gets close to your time to leave this world you will know in your heart that you have given all you could toward your personal soul growth and with that effort, God will be pleased.

The goddess in me greets the goddess in you and wishes you good luck on your road of life.

JMC 12/02/2005

ENDNOTES

1   Edgar Cayce, Story of the Origin and Destiny of Man by Lytle Robinson, Copyright 1972, the Edgar Cayce Foundation, (New York, N.Y.:Berkley Publishing Corporation):29-41

2   Said by Elayne Khan in an article by Susan Evans, The Way You Part Your Hair Reveals the Real You! Weekly World News, October 2, 2001, (Boca Raton,FL.: American Media Consumer Entertainment, 2001):5.

3   Study by Sally Fry and Rosalind Craig, in an article by Millie Spencer, Hold Your Man's Hand and Read Him Like a Book, Weekly World News, December 17, 1991, (Boca Raton, FL.:American Media Consumer Entertainment, 1991):45.

4   Adapted from lists of herbal teas, by Jethro Kloss, Back to Eden, revised and expanded Second Edition, Kloss Family, copyright 1991 (Loma Linda, CA.:Back to Eden Publishing Co.):261.

5   Spiced Tea, Irma S. Rombauer and Marion Rombauer Becker, Joy of Cooking, (Indianapolis, IN.: the Bobbs-Merrill Co. 1964):29.

6   Ginger Tea, adapted from Sensational Summer Sippers by Molly O'Neill, Reader's Digest, June 2005 (Pleasantville, N.Y.: Reader's Digest):182.

7   Mint Tea, from the Cook's Encyclopedia of Herbs by Andi Clevely and Katherine Richmond, (New York, N.Y.: Anness Publishing Inc. 2001):204.

8   Standard Muffin Mixes from Irma S. Rombauer and Marion Rombauer Becker, Joy of Cooking,

(Indianapolis, IN.: the Bobbs-Merrill Co., 1964):580-581

[9] Rosemary Bread from the Cook's Encyclopedia of Herbs by Andi Clevely and Katherine Richmond, (New York, N.Y.: Anness Publishing Inc. 2001):1

SUGGESTED READING

1. Reader's Digest Great Health Hints & Handy Tips, more then 4,000 Ideas to Help You Look and Feel Your Best. Copyright 1994, (Pleasantville, N.Y.: Reader's Digest) ISBN 0-89577-619-7.
2. Feng Shui for Beginners, copyright 1997 by Richard Webster (Eighth printing 2004), (St. Paul, MN: Llewellyn Publications) ISBN 1-56718-803-6.
3. Sun Signs by Linda Goodman 1968, (New York, N.Y.:Taplinger Publishing Co., 1968) and (New York, N.Y.: Bantam Books, 1971) ISBN 0553-02777-8.
4. The Everything Reflexology Book by Valerie Voner CRT., CTM., RMT., (Avon, MA: Adams Media Corp. 2003) ISBN 07394-4159-0.
5. Great Sex Games by Anne Hooper, (London and New York: Dorling Kindersley Ltd, 2000) ISBN 07894-6837-9.
6. The Kama Sutra by Anne Hooper, (London and New York: Dorling Kindersley Ltd. 2000) ISBN 07894-5072-0.
7. The Bedside Kama Sutra, 23 Positions for Pleasure and Passion, by Linda Sonntag, copyright 2001 Octopus Publishing Group Ltd. (Gloucester, MA: Fair Winds Press 2001) ISBN 1-931412-79-0.
8. The complete Idiot's Guide to Tantric Sex, Second Edition, by Dr. Judy Kuriansky, copyright 2004, Dr. Judy Kuriansky (New York, N.Y.: Penguin Group) ISBN 1-59257-296-0.
9. The Kama Sutra of Vatsayayana trans. by Richard Burton from Wikipedia at: http://en.wikipedia.org/wiki/kamasutra.

BIBLIOGRAPHY

1. Burton, Richard (transulator) The Kama Sutra of Vatsayayana, wikipedia, the free encyclopedia, at: http://en.wikipedia.org/wiki/kamasutra (retrieved 9/13/2005).
2. Clevely, Andi and Katherine Richmond, the Cook's Encyclopedia of Herbs, New York, N.Y.:Anness Publishing 2001:194 and 204.
3. Evans, Susan, The Way You Part Your Hair Reveals the Real You! Weekly World News, October 2, 2001, Boca Raton, FL.: American Media Consumer Entertainment 2001:5.
4. Gamber, Garry, The Language and Meaning of Flowers, www.kansascuties.com/articles/the-language-and-meaning-of-flowers.shtml. History pg 1-2 (retrieved 10/1/2005) and Meaning and list pg 2-6 (retrived 9/29/2005).
5. Goodman, Linda, Sun Signs, copyright 1968 by Linda Goodman, New York, N.Y.: Taplinger Publishing Co. Inc. 1968 and a Bantam Book 1971: xviii.
6. Hsu-Le Blanc, Elisabeth, What Men Really Need, Taste for Life, June 2005, Peterborough, NH.: CCI, 2005:24-26.
7. Kumar, Nitin, Tantra: the Art of Philosophy, copyright 2000, Exotic India Art, September 2001:3. Found at: http://www.exoticindia.com.
8. Kuriansky, Dr. Judy, The Complete Idiot's Guide to Tantric Sex, Second Edition, copyright 2004 by Dr. Judy Kuriansky, New York, N.Y.: the Penguin Group, 2004:2,36 and 48.

9. Jimson, Susan, Make Your Sex Life Sizzle – by Changing Your Diet, Weekly World News, September 29, 1992, Boca Raton, FL.: American Media Consumer Entertainment, 1992:38.

10. Jimson, Susan, Sex Trivia, Weekly World News, December 17, 1991, Boca Raton, FL.: American Media Consumer Entertainment, 1991:29.

11. Kloss, Jethro, Back to Eden, Second Edition, copyright 1995, Kloss Family, Loma Linda, CA.: Back to Eden Publishing Co. 1995:68-69, 261 and 516.

12. O'Neill, Molly, Sensational Summer Sippers, Reader's Digest, June 2005, Pleasantville, N.Y.: Reader's Digest 2005:182.

13. Reader's Digest, Great Health Hints & Handy Tips: more than 4,000 Ideas to Help You Look and Feel Your Best, copyright 1994, Pleasantville, N.Y.: Reader's Digest, 1994:12-17, 38-45, 88-89, 120-123, 130-139, 144-145, 188 and 336.

14. Robinson, Lytle, Edgar Cayce's Story of the Origin and Destiny of Man, copyright 1972 by the Edgar Cayce Foundation a Berkley Medallion Book, New York, N.Y.: Berkley Publishing Corporation 1976 edition:28-41.

15. Rombauer, Irma S. and Marion Rombauer Becker, Joy of Cooking copyright 1964, Indianapolis, IN.: the Bobbs-Merrill Co. Inc.:29, 580 and 581.

16. Spencer, Millie, Hold Your Man's Hand and Read Him Like a Book, Weekly World News, December 17, 1991, Boca Raton, FL.: American Media Consumer Entertainment 1991:45.

17. Voner, Valerie, CRT., CTM., RMT., The Everything Reflexology Book, copyright 2003, Avon, MA.: Adams Media Corporation 2003:52-53, 59-61.

18. Webster, Richard Feng Shui for Beginners, copyright 1997, Richard Webster, (Eighth Printing 2004) St. Paul, MN.: Llewellyn Publishing 2004:1-7.
19. Ginkgo biloba, Herbal Focus, Sue's Health Foods, Health Notes Newsletter, Summer 1998, Portland, OR.: Norma Hunt copyright 1998 Vitual Health LLC:3.

Biblical Quotes
20. Imperial Reference Bible with Concordance, The New King James version, copyright 1983, New York, N.Y.: Thomas Nelson Publishers: all quotes marked by book and passage.

Boxed Poems
21. Conrow, Judith Morland, each poem is dated when written.